Gluten-Free

in

LIZARD LICK

Gluten-Free
in
LIZARD LICK

100 Gluten-Free Recipes
for Finger-Licking Food for Your Soul

Amy Shirley

HarperOne
An Imprint of HarperCollinsPublishers

HarperOne

HarperCollins books may be purchased for educational, business, or sales promotional use. For information please e-mail the Special Markets Department at SPsales@harpercollins.com.

HarperCollins website: http://www.harpercollins.com

HarperCollins®, ®, and HarperOne™ are trademarks of HarperCollins Publishers.

FIRST EDITION

Designed by Shelly Peppel/Cookbooks365.com
Recipe photographs courtesy of William Chambers
Recipe photograph styling by Karen Morgan
Lifestyle photographs courtesy of Tammy Robbins

Library of Congress Cataloging-in-Publication Data

Shirley, Amy.
  Gluten-free in lizard lick : 100 gluten-free recipes for finger-licking food for your
soul / Amy Shirley.
        p. cm.
    ISBN 978-0-06-238398-3
    1. Gluten-free diet—Recipes. 2. Cooking, American—Southern style. 3. Cooking—Southern
States. I. Title.
    RM237.86.S544 2015
    641.5'638—dc23   2014042030

15 16 17 18 19 RRD(H) 10 9 8 7 6 5 4 3 2 1

Just because you're country-fried doesn't mean you can't eat gluten-free without your neighbor talking smack about ya.

Contents

Introduction

Why I Left the Gluten

If I was a betting woman, I would bet you second-guessed what you were seeing when you saw this book just now. I bet you did a double take. I bet you said, "Amy Shirley is gluten-free?" so loud the person next to you asked what you were talking about. Most people don't know I'm gluten-free, but you can butter my butt and call me a gluten-free biscuit. I am as gluten-free as they come.

Around here in North Carolina, we just shell the corn down and you know, tell it like it is. So I'm gonna tell you like it is. Before this book, before me going away from the gluten, I was a gluten lover just like the rest of you all. I ate gluten morning, noon, and night, except when I was training for my next power-lifting competition. I ate gluten on the set of *Lizard Lick Towing*, and I ate it with every slice of pizza and free sample they handed to me when I was running errands at Costco with my kids. Let's face it, y'all, we all go to Costco to make a lunch of those samples.

Before I left the gluten, I was just living my Lizard Licking life the way Ronnie and I always did, until one day everything started to change. I didn't know what it was, but all the sudden, I got sick. Real sick. So sick, I thought I was going to die. My doctors told me I had all the symptoms for blood cancer (leukemia): I lost twenty pounds in a little over a month, which is a big deal for me because I don't lose weight easy; I love to eat! I couldn't go to the bathroom to save my life (yes, number two), my hands swelled up, and my joints, from my ankles to my shoulders, screamed in pain. And the night sweats? Oh, sweet lord of mercy, those night sweats were the worst! I would sweat in the night so bad I would wake up with gallons of water all over my body. Worst of all, though, I started bruising like a peach. If Ronnie hugged me too hard, I'd have a bruise on my arm the next day. It was absolutely the worst I'd ever felt in my life.

This went on for a couple of months, and then it got worse. No matter what, after we'd eat dinner, even if it was something simple like my Over-the-Sink BLT (page 91), I would spend the night doubled over in pain, sweating on my bathroom floor. I'd never been in so much pain, even when I was in labor with my children! Only the Lord knows how much pain I was in. I became desperate to figure out what the heck was going on, so I started asking my doctor questions, and lots of them. It was tough going.

I remember one night I was lying on my hardwood floor. I had taken my shirt off because the inside of my body felt like it was on fire. My stomach was bloated, so I looked like I was about three months pregnant. It was about 30 degrees outside and I had the door wide open just so that I could feel like I could breathe. My husband was looking at me, asking, "Do you want me to call 911?" And I said, "If I pass out in the next thirty seconds, call."

I was so upset, I nearly moved into my doctor's office just so we could get to the bottom of what the deal was a little faster. My doctor, thank goodness, was real patient with me, because even he couldn't figure out what was happening. So he drew my blood and tested it, and he drew more blood and tested that. He went on like this until finally one day he said, "You know what, Amy? I'm going to send you to a gastroenterologist because all the tests I've done on you are coming back negative, so I think you might have some food allergies."

So I followed my doctor's orders and went to the gastro guy. He drew some more blood from me. Then he looked me square in the eye and said, "I don't know how to tell you, so I'll just say it. You are allergic to sulfides, gluten, and cocoa, and you are sensitive to sugar."

After my face melted off and I scooped it up off the floor, he told me my body now hated gluten with a passion and attacks it every time I eat it, and it was gonna keep on attacking until my day is done. So I had two options: Give up the gluten and live without the pain, without the swelling, without the night sweats, without the easy bruising, and at my normal healthy weight, or keep eating the gluten and endure all the pain and suffering that goes with it. It was right then and there that my days with the gluten were done. I knew I didn't really have any other choice, but I gotta say, I was upset because I ate so much gluten and I really didn't know what all it was in. Long story short, I was scared worse than a deer in the headlights. So I took a big deep breath and held it in for a moment, and as I held that breath, I sat with his words. By the time I let that breath out, my gut agreed that there was a war going on inside me and all I wanted was for it to stop.

"Now, Doc, let me see if I got this straight. Are you meaning to tell me that what has made me this sick is *food*? Are you sure? I mean, I just don't understand how food could be doing this to me. It's food I've eaten my whole life. How in the heck is this possible?"

"Well, Amy, this is something we see a lot of these days, but most people don't want to hear that the food they are eating is killing them," he said. Of course, this went over like Madea trying to do yoga.

Then I stared at him with my mouth open just enough that he could tell I was in shock. "Doc, are you telling me that I pretty much have to relearn how to eat?"

"Yes, Amy, that is exactly what I am saying. You are going to need to take a few things to get your insides back on track, but other than that, you are going to heal yourself with the food you eat."

"Doc, didn't a famous philosopher say that?" I asked.

"Yes, it was a real, real old guy named Hippocrates, and he said, 'Let food be thy medicine.'" He smiled. And I know he was smiling because he would have never guessed I knew that one.

Anyhow, that is how I came to leave the gluten behind, but actually leaving it on the curb wasn't easy at all. Heck, repo-ing a car is way easier than giving up the gluten. But even after I knew it was bad, I had to teach myself how to look for the red flags everywhere I went. I spent hours—*hours*—at the grocery store and Target just standing in the aisles reading labels. I mean, I read everything and started seeing words like *xanthan gum* and *modified food starch* and didn't know what the heck it meant. It was frustrating because not only am I a working mother of four that happens to have a TV show, I also travel all the time, meaning I don't have a lot of extra time to stand there reading what's in this or that. I had to talk to someone who knew a thing or two about gluten so I could spend less time at the store obsessing about every little thing I put in my basket and could get home to my family.

I put in a call to my lawyer, who called his lady friend, Karen Morgan. Talking to her was like having the heavens open up, and for the first time in months, I started to feel like there was light at the end of the tunnel. Seeing the world through her eyes was like putting on glasses. I told her how crazy I felt and how my life was basically in an uproar since I had to give up gluten and I didn't know what to do.

Not only was I aggravated about doing simple things like grocery shopping, but I told her I didn't know why my skin was breaking out worse than when I was a teenager.

"Oh, the same thing happened to me when I went gluten-free," she said. "It's because there is gluten in your makeup and it makes your face break out like a pepperoni pizza. You have to change everything, from the lotion that you use to the soap you wash your hands with."

"Are you serious?" I asked. I had no idea. Gluten was in my makeup? Yes, it is. Gluten is in my lotion and in my shampoo? Yes, it is—my shampoo, soaps, makeup. (Even today sometimes I want to buy something and I get home and put it on my face and my face will break out. I'm like, well, that was a dumb move.)

Karen knew things my doctors didn't know, and pretty much everything she told me blew my mind. Needless to say, my blinders were off and I was in shock. Heck, I never thought something as simple as gluten could have such an impact on my life.

Now, if I told you a rooster could pull a freight train, you better hook it up, and I'm telling you, in less than an hour, not only did she convince me I wasn't crazy, she gave me a list of trusted gluten-free products I could start buying right away (see the resource section on page 199 for the list she sent to me), and told me what the red flags are so I could start spending a lot less time reading at the store.

The biggest red flags, she told me, were modified food starch, soy sauce, mono-sodium glutamate, malt extract, malt flavoring, and caramel color. All these things meant that gluten was in there, so run from it like the plague. Xanthan gum is a kind of glue and is in pretty much every single gluten-free product, but she said I should avoid xanthan gum when I first go gluten-free because it can make a person have the same kind of reaction as eating the gluten.

I would have had to spend years reading to find out what I learned from her in that short phone call. I had to look at every product in my life, and because I am so sensitive, it took six months to feel a big improvement, and a year for me to feel fully well and get all of the gluten gunk out of my body. It's just like I always say, you can't always be the first to find out, but you can dang sure be the next. And truth be told, it was that phone call that changed my life again, but this time for the better.

**The most common way people give up their power
is thinking they don't have any.**
— *Alice Walker*

You Can't Have It Your Way Right Away, but You Sure Can Love It

What people do know about Amy Shirley is that I am the better half of Ronnie Shirley on the hit TV reality show *Lizard Lick Towing*, but I'm much more than that. I am also the proud mother to my four children, Alexa, Alex, Gabe, and Maggie, and am a twenty-seven-time world power-lifter champion. Being married to Ronnie is certainly wilder than a hog chase, but when it comes down to it, we are a very close-knit family, and when the cameras aren't rolling, everything we do is about spending time together. Each of my kids has a favorite meal of mine that I make just for him or her, so can you imagine my shock when I was told I couldn't eat the gluten anymore?

In my mind, all I could think about is how messy our supper table was going to be. I know my kids, and I know they wouldn't in a million years eat things without the gluten in it because a lot of the stuff out there doesn't taste anything close to good. And then there is Ronnie.

Trust me when I tell you that Ronnie nearly had a heart attack when I told him I couldn't eat gluten anymore. "Hold up, Amy. Just hold up. So what you are saying is that you can't eat wheat, like the stuff that makes bread and everything else on God's green earth taste good? Well, what the heck, Amy! What are we gonna do? Baby, *what* are we gonna eat? Oh Lord, don't you die on me!" I mean, he went on like this for a full half hour. After I thought to myself that this man is the reason they invented Xanax, I knew that I had to make my situation better, not just for me, but for my family and all the people that watch *Lizard Lick Towing*. Whenever life gives me a challenge, I always think to myself, I can step to the left, I can step to the right, or I can step up, and this whole gluten-free thing told me it was time to step up.

Stepping up meant I had to get into the kitchen, and since I didn't know the first thing about baking or cooking gluten-free, I gave Karen a call for some much-needed pointers.

"Hello?"

"Hey, Karen, it's Amy."

"How's it going, Amy? Are you feeling any better?" she asked.

"Oh, I'm doing great, but I would be a whole lot better if I could make my mama's 1-2-3-4 Cake gluten-free. I know you can't fix stupid, but can you help make it better?" I asked.

After she laughed her big Texas laugh, we got right to work and I explained to her that when I'm feeling down, the only thing that cheers me up is a piece of cake, and since I'd gone gluten-free, I hadn't had a good piece of gluten-free cake in months. She said she could help, and I believed her. Then I told her how I wanted to make gluten-free as easy as possible for myself since I was so dang busy all the time, and she got me a solution the very next week. She sent me a recipe conversion of my mama's famous 1-2-3-4 Cake, along with a bag that said *Amy's Gluten-Free Mix* on the front. I was so excited, I went ahead and rolled up my shirtsleeves and put both the mix and the recipe to the test.

I plugged in my Cadillac mixer and started whipping the butter and the sugar, and everything felt just like when I was a little girl. Okay, the butter and the sugar look the same, but what's gonna happen when I add the gluten-free flour mix? I kept working my way through the recipe. I added the eggs. No explosions, so I was doing good. Everything was exactly the same as when I was little, with one difference. Instead of regular all-purpose flour, I had me a gluten-free flour mix with my name on it. So I sifted the flour into the bowl, mixed it in good, crossed my fingers, and then poured the batter into the pans. I'd be lying if I told you I wasn't nervous, because I was. I was so nervous, I crossed my fingers and my eyelashes, pulled up my kitchen chair, and waited.

The Original 1-2-3-4 Cake

Serves 6

**Unsalted butter
for greasing pan**

**1 cup (2 sticks)
unsalted butter**

2 cups sugar

4 large eggs

3 cups flour

4 teaspoons baking powder

½ teaspoon salt

1 cup milk

2 tablespoons vanilla extract

**Amy's Buttercream Icing
(page 10)**

Preheat the oven to 350°F. Grease two 9-inch round cake pans with unsalted butter and line with parchment paper on the bottom.

In the bowl of a stand mixer with a paddle attachment, whip the butter with the sugar. Add the eggs and whip until light and fluffy. Next sift in the flour, baking powder, and salt. Mix on high until nice and smooth. Add the milk and the vanilla extract last, mixing just until smooth.

Divide the batter between the two pans, level the dough with a spatula, and bake for 20 to 25 minutes, rotating the pans halfway through, from top to bottom, so they bake evenly. The cakes are done when a toothpick comes out clean and the cakes pull away from the sides of the pan slightly.

Allow to cool in the pan for 10 minutes, then invert onto a wire rack to finish cooling off.

Now make my super-simple Buttercream Icing (page 10).

After the cakes have cooled, place one cake round on a plate or stand. Ice just the top of the cake. Add the other cake round top side down, and then ice the rest of the cake with the icing.

Slice and serve. Will keep on my kitchen counter for a day or so, but that's only because it gets eaten. Tastes great out of the fridge late at night!

NOTES:

_____

_____

_____

Amy's Buttercream Icing

3 cups confectioners' sugar

½ cup (1 stick)
unsalted butter

1 to 3 tablespoons milk

1 teaspoon vanilla extract

1 teaspoon butter-flavored
extract

In your mixer with the paddle attachment, cream the butter with the sugar until you can't see the butter no more. Add the milk one tablespoon at a time, being sure to whip on high until super smooth after each addition. I usually add about 2½ tablespoons of milk. Add the vanilla and butter-flavored extracts and mix just until combined. The icing should be thick but spreadable. If it isn't, add a little more milk until it is.

NOTES:

_____

_____

_____

_____

_____

_____

When the cakes came out of the oven, they looked exactly the same as my mama's. I took the cakes out of the pans, and the cakes were perfect. I mean, golden and perfect. I could believe it, but since it had been so long since I'd had a piece of cake, I was pretty darn giddy, so I pinched myself to make sure I wasn't sleepwalking.

I whipped up the buttercream icing in a flash and iced that cake like nobody's business. I got out my favorite knife and cut into the cake. The knife went right through it. No sawing, no pushing, no squishing; the knife did what it was supposed to do and it cut a perfectly soft piece of cake. Oh my lord, that first slice I will never forget. The cake was buttery and moist just as it had been when we'd eat it in the front yard when I was a teenager, and it was gluten-free! Looking back, I know it was that piece of cake that was the turning point for me, because after not being able to have something for six very long months, my taste buds were doing backflips. I would even say that I was ecstatic. And you know Ronnie had something to say about it. Granted, this was coming from someone that has managed to burn boiling water, but I still knew what he meant.

"Baby, you know what, this is so good, it reminds me of your mama's 1-2-3-4 Cake!"

"That's what it is. Duh." I smiled.

"No way! Are you saying you made your mama's 1-2-3-4 Cake gluten-free?" he asked.

"I did!" I smiled as I jabbed a finger between his ribs.

Then we looked at each other and I swear it was like that thermometer that pops out of a Thanksgiving turkey; we both had the same idea at the same time. I needed to make all my favorite recipes gluten-free and then share them with my fans. Everyone deserves to be able to eat delicious, healthy meals, but in order to do that, we all need a little know-how.

So I got to work and started making my list. Okay, I made a few lists, because I wanted to make sure I included all my *favorite* breakfasts, lunches, snacks for the in-between times, suppers, and desserts. Before I knew it, I had over a hundred recipes when I put all those lists together, and all together I suddenly had a book. But I'd never written a book before, so I called Karen up again.

"Hey," I said.

"Hey, lady, what's shakin'?" Karen asked.

"Remember that idea I had about doing a gluten-free cookbook?"

"Yeah."

"Well, it just so happens that I am staring at a list of over a hundred recipes. What do you think? Are you in or were you just joshing?" I smiled, even though she couldn't see me.

"Does the pope wear a funny hat?"

And that, my friends, is how we popped the clutch on this cookbook.

If the Kids Will Eat It,
You Know You Are Doing Something Right

Remember how I was saying my kids wouldn't try gluten-free in a million years because they figured it wouldn't taste good? Well, when I started sneaking my gluten-free recipes for this book onto the table, they were like, "Wow, Mom, this is gluten-free? It's really good!"

"Dang straight it's good! Didn't your mama just put it on the table?"

Ronnie is my biggest baby of all. I mean, if he hears "gluten-free," his face freezes and his eyes get big as a pair of saucers. That is of course until he started eating my old standards in their gluten-free form. Now even he is on the gluten-free wagon with me, at least most of the time. Like when I make DJ Silver's Spicy Fried Pickles (page 106) and Alexa's Best Ever Meatloaf (page 140), but those are just a few examples. Depending on the weather and depending on what we are in the mood for, I can make any one of these recipes and my whole family will be happy as hobo on a ham sandwich.

What adult or child wants to just eat vegetables and meat after going gluten-free? I could probably live that way; it's the caveman diet. I could probably eat Paleo if I put my mind to it, but I don't know a child who would eat that way every day. And I love sweets just as much as the next person.

Anyhow, as you work your way through my book, the most important thing to remember when you are making these recipes for your family is to keep the kiddos happy, because there is nothing worse than having to work like a dog all day and then come home to a house full of upset kids. Luckily, all the recipes in this book passed the hungry kid test, so no matter how old your kids are, you really can't go wrong. Even when those kids are as old as Ronnie.

A Day in the Life of Eating Gluten-Free with Amy Shirley

One day out of my life is certainly no rodeo, but it ain't like watching paint dry either. It's somewhere in between. Plenty of crazy, but that's just because there aren't enough hours in the day to get everything done. When I wake up, it's usually before everyone else to make sure the kids have something to eat before they get off to school. Since they are not 100 percent gluten-free like me, sometimes they eat a gluten-free breakfast and sometimes they don't. All I care is that they are fed and fed well before they get going.

Then I get dressed and make my old standby breakfast: eggs any way I please and turkey bacon. I'm a creature of habit and can eat the same thing over and over for certain meals; during the week, I have eggs and turkey bacon just about every day. The weekends are a different story. Then I make my lunch before heading into the Lizard Lick Towing office. What I bring in totally depends on whether or not we are filming.

Filming is exhausting because you are always "on." The best way to describe what this means is comparing my energy brain to a lightbulb. When the bulb is on, it's glowing as bright as possible, and when the filming stops, that lightbulb (my brain) becomes totally exhausted, so eating healthy to keep that bulb burning bright is super important. It's true we do have a craft service table on the set of *Lizard Lick Towing,* but it hardly ever has anything gluten-free, so I always bring my own food. Even if they promise me that everything is gluten-free, I'm always terrified of cross-contamination, so I always just bring my own lunch so I don't get sick, because when I get any of the gluten in my stomach, I get so sick, I am down for days, and I just don't have time to be down for that long.

A typical lunch for me can be anything from my Power-Lifter Grilled Chicken Salad (page 86) to my Tuna Salad (page 97) or my Every-Time Chicken Salad (page 77). Something that travels well and has plenty of protein keeps me going for the whole day.

When it's time to head home, I get my grocery list ready and head to the store (be sure to check out the list of resources I have in the back of the book, page 197). When I first went gluten-free, this part of my day used to take forever, and I'd find myself rolling into the driveway when it was well after dark. Now I can get in and out of the store with my gluten-free goodies in nothing flat. Going gluten-free is like anything else. It takes practice to get your system down.

For dinner, I like to make a good hot dish (and you will see many recipes for casseroles throughout the book) for the family because it's a nice large portion and it leaves everyone fuller and happier than a fat tick on a lazy dog. I've gotta say my Gluten-Free Hamburger Helper (page 149) is a real winner when the kids are so hungry, because to heck with seconds—how about thirds, fourths, and fifths?

Truth be told, however, we do have nights when we have a mixed table. Some of the things are gluten-free while others have gluten so my kids don't get all bent out of shape on me.

Luckily Alexa and Maggie will eat anything gluten-free, but Alex and Gabe are another story. I love them all so much, I really don't care either way, just so long as my kids always know they are loved by me and Ronnie. One of the best lessons I've learned as a mother of four is you have to learn how to choose your battles, and sometimes fighting over food just ain't worth it. Two wrongs don't make a right. Lucky for me (and you!), our household is slowly becoming a gluten-free one because the recipes in this book are just that good, and my daughter Maggie, I swear I think she is going to become a chef. That girl is cooking or baking every single day!

Now, another day in my life is when we cook on the set of *Lizard Lick Towing.* And let me tell you, this is no small production. When we go hog-wild, we cook the whole hog. Literally. Last time we cooked for the cast and crew of the show, Ronnie had a pig pickin', in which he stops the roasting pig from rotating every 20 minutes and drenches the whole pig in Pop's Eastern North Carolina Lizard Lick Barbeque Sauce, and it cooks for about 8 hours. For the recipe check out page 18.

The Whole Hog

Makes enough for 100

1 young pig
(at least 90 pounds
and no more than 170)

25 pounds charcoal

Coarse salt

**Pop's Eastern North Carolina
Lizard Lick Barbeque Sauce**

Slow-roasting a pig is a lot of fun because it can feed so many people and it tastes so darn good. I mean, you only need salt, a cooker, and some charcoal and you are good to go.

We always use a pig that is at least 90 pounds and no more than 170, because when a pig gets above that weight, it carries excess fat and it takes longer to cook and does not hold the sauce as well. So rather than stress ourselves out, Ronnie and I always stick with the lucky number eleven and get one around 110 pounds.

If you want to know how to build a pig cooker, just call Ronnie or Pops. They can tell you how to build one blindfolded.

Anyhow, to roast a juicy pig, you need to get started early. And I mean the butt crack of dawn early, because it will take you a good 8 hours to roast a pig. Ronnie always tells me, "Remember, baby, this pig ain't strong like you, I can break it down in eight hours. I still haven't broken you and we've been together since . . . too long." Isn't he romantic? Ha ha.

Where was I? Oh yeah, the pig. So you take the pig and lay him out on Ronnie's custom grill cooker. The pig is whole but laid out flat so it can to rotate. Once it's in place, slowly turn it. Every 20 minutes, add sauce. The last hour, leave the skin side down, until the skin is crispy enough to eat. This is just like grabbing a bag of pork skins at the gas station, except these are fresh off the grill. Yummy. My stomach is already growling.

Easy, right? I just love a good pig roast. Not just because it tastes so good, but because it gives us a chance to visit with our family and friends. And believe me when I tell you that when you film a TV show, that whole crew becomes a part of your family. Like it or not!

NOTES:

_____
_____
_____
_____
_____
_____
_____
_____
_____
_____
_____
_____
_____
_____
_____
_____
_____
_____
_____
_____
_____
_____

The Cat's Out of the Bag

Let's Get Gluten-Free Licking in Lizard Lick, North Carolina

Can you tell I'm a talker? Ronnie always says I'm a go-getter, but not a follow-upper, so I'm gonna prove him wrong and follow up with what I was sayin'. We were talking about how I got my mind set on doing a gluten-free cookbook. Well, for starters, the fact that I am writing this cookbook in the first place is a total shocker, because never in my life did I ever think that I would be eating gluten-free. But life unfolds in ways that we will never understand, and usually in ways that lead us to where we were always meant to be. For me, that just so happened to be barefoot in the kitchen with Ronnie's mono-ab belly staring at me, asking for breakfast. This going away from gluten happened to me after I had my second child, when I already knew what all my favorite foods tasted like. So to have someone tell me I can't have this and that was like taking chocolate away from a baby.

As adults, we're already set in our ways, so going away from gluten was tough as nails for me. Tough at first. Then I saw the opportunity for me to do what every adult hates most: change. I just reminded myself that if I didn't change, I'd stay sick as a dog, and remembering that fact made it easy again. Plus, I'm always looking to find solutions to problems. I like to shake things up, to make something different, and honestly, make it easier. That's another reason why I wanted to do this cookbook. Nobody wants to stand at a freakin' kitchen stove to cook a meal for an hour after she's gotten home from work and taken the kids to dance or football. You've got to have something easy, something you enjoy that's healthy for you. And you need to be able to find the ingredients without going on Google to research them first. My four-year-old will eat anything 'cause Mom does. But my nine-year-old is the final test of a recipe. He'll ask me if something is gluten-free and I'll ask, "What do you think?" And when he says, "No way, it tastes too good to be gluten-free!" I know I've done good. There is nothing I love more than making others happy.

Which is a part of me that most people don't know too much about. Helping others is the most important thing to me, and if it isn't my family, it's the stranger on the street, because I also know that when you give back, life just feels more full. It makes your heart feel good. So, after learning everything I learned since going gluten-free, I wanted to share all this newness with anyone that cared to listen. I don't care who you are. It doesn't matter where you live, what job you have, or what kind of friends you surround yourself with. As long as you can smile at a stranger and know how to make a good fried pickle, you're as good as gold in my book. No matter what walk of life you come from, we all have one thing in common: We all have to eat, so pull up a chair and stay a while. I'll teach you how to make a perfect gluten-free fried pickle (page 106) and one of my favorite gestures of friendship in the world, the lemon poppy seed muffin (page 44).

Some people call me a cheapskate, but that's just another word for thrifty or clever, so don't start sweating just yet. Karen and I worked hard to make sure that this book was tailor-made so as not to empty out every last coffee can in the house. I came from next to nothing, so I don't take anything for granted and still use ingredients I used before *Lizard Lick Towing* came into our lives. I still love to eat Spam, and I still use canned cream of mushroom soup to make my hot dishes (that's country for casserole).

You'll see plenty of recipes that begin with a can opener and end with a microwave, so you better start watching the Home Shopping Network now if you don't have either of these. You will also see recipes with all kinds of fresh veggies, farm-fresh eggs, and sausage made up by our friend Randy. (Everyone needs a friend that knows how to make homemade sausage!)

In fact, most of the recipes in this book are what I like to call microwave babies. Some of them are actually made in the microwave, while others are just super simple to make and can be done in less than 30 minutes. Other recipes, like Donna D's Honey'd Oat Bread (page 58), take a pinch more time, but that is because not even I can rush bread, but we all need bread to live, so I was sure to include a recipe for all you bread bakers. Sorry, I don't have a recipe for candlesticks.

No matter what, don't fret over a single recipe because to your family and friends, you will look like a genius. It doesn't matter what other people think. It's like I always say: Remember, you're a genius, only different.

The First Step to Licking the Gluten
My Gluten-Free Mix

I know right now you are feeling all roostered up, but hold on before you start releasing your cock-a-doodle-doo and get your kitchen in a hot mess. There are a couple of things you need to get in order before you pounce. The most important thing is my flour mix that Karen made up for me. It's as easy as pie to make, and you can store it in an airtight container for up to a year.

The trick to making all my favorite recipes gluten-free was coming up with a mix of gluten-free flours and starches that would imitate regular all-purpose flour. Watching me try to come up with a gluten-free mix that would do just that would be like me trying to nail raw egg to an oak tree, so I left that up to Karen. Have you ever seen that movie *Back to the Future*? Karen is like the mad scientist, Doc, minus the lab coat and the bad hair. Anyhow, me trying to explain all the nitty-gritty reasons why this mix is the way that it is would be the same as watching my grandma trying to run uphill in combat boots. Are you catching my drift? Some things are better left to the experts. It's like my grandma always said: "Know what you don't know so you can surround yourself with the people that do."

As Karen says, though, this here mix sure is good for you because it's got so much good stuff in it. The guar gum adds fiber and helps regulate your blood sugar, and the millet has more protein in it than a power lifter's breakfast.

You can get all the ingredients at your local health-food store, like Whole Foods, or at Kroger. Or if you're standing in the right spot, you can pick up a bag of my ready-made mix and skip this part altogether!

Oh, and don't let the name of the rice flour fool you. Glutinous rice flour is just made with sushi rice, so it has a better texture than the other rice flours out there and is extremely cheap—only about a dollar a pound at most local Asian markets.

Amy's Gluten-Free Mix

2 cups millet flour

2 cups glutinous rice flour

1 cup tapioca starch

⅔ cup + 2 tablespoons cornstarch

6 tablespoons potato starch

6 teaspoons guar gum

This will make just under 6 cups of my mix. Combine all ingredients and store in an airtight container for up to a year.

NOTES:

My Gluten-Free Kitchen Rules

When I began to cook gluten-free, through trial and error I discovered that everything in my kitchen was contaminated. I just didn't know it. I'd eat something and start to get a small stomachache and wonder why I felt so bad. All I knew was that I should not be hurting. It wasn't that I was going into a severe attack, but something just wasn't right. If I eat a little bit it's going to affect me but not throw me fully into "I can't breathe" territory. But I slowly realized every time that happened I'd done something to cross-contaminate my food. For example, when I make spaghetti, the sauce and the meat are gluten-free, and I make one batch of noodles that is gluten-free and one that is not. (I like to give my kids the choice.) Everything is kept separate, but without exception, whenever I did something simple like use the same spoon to stir the different pastas while they're cooking, I paid for it later.

As a result, I have separate silverware for myself and I don't even let my kids take sips out of my cup. My husband has seen me change and watched me put all this effort into keeping things separate. So now if he has a slice of pizza he'll actually be so thoughtful as to go brush his teeth and wash his face before coming over to kiss me. It's really good. Most people don't think about that. Same thing should go for people with peanut allergies. If you just had a peanut butter sandwich and then head over to give a child a hug, you'd never think you're going to hurt him or her, but you could. I think it's tough for people to get because it's an internal issue; they can't see the problem on the outside.

But back to my kitchen, I like being organized and anything I do I give 100 percent. So it's simpler for me just to separate things. It's not like you have to go out and get brand-new things. You can put your gadgets and pots and pans in the dishwasher, power-wash them, take them out, and let them air-dry. But some things make life easier. For example, I have a four-slice toaster. On two sides the kids can cook their gluten stuff and on two sides I can cook my gluten-free stuff. Don't put that other stuff in mine! I have it labeled!

KITCHEN GADGETS

1. My Cadillac mixer
(KitchenAid Stand Mixer I bought using my frequent-flier miles)

2. Brightly colored spreaders for the kids

3. My blender

4. Big ol' spoons: wooden spoons and stainless are my favorite

5. Stainless steel anything

6. My cast-iron skillet
This right here wears the crown as the single most important item in my kitchen. You can get them just about anywhere these days, but I got mine from my mama years ago. I like a good 10- or 12-inch skillet. They may be heavy and clunky—and if you touch the handle without a dishcloth or oven mitt you'll be hurtin'—but keep your skillet properly seasoned and get ready to make some of the best bacon of all time. Remember these were made tough enough for open fire cooking, and they'll heat up evenly and stay that way long after the cows come home. See the next page for more tips.

Cast-Iron Skillet TLC

Seasoning

If you take care of your cast-iron skillet, it will be your friend for life and for your children's lives and beyond, too, just like my mama's is to me. People love them these days because they're nonstick without any of the toxic coatings that are out there. (Yet another example of the old-timey ways ending up on top again.) Originally you'd get a new cast-iron skillet totally unseasoned and you'd have to start from scratch, but if you aren't lucky enough to inherit a preseasoned one, some out-of-the-box cast-iron cookware, like American-made Lodge cookware, comes that way now anyway. The trick is to keep it in good shape once you've got it. One way to season a new pan is to coat it with cooking oil. (I don't use olive oil to season my pan—only high-heat oils like vegetable oil or grape-seed oil.) Then bake the pan in the oven at 350°F for an hour or so. Give it a wipe-down and it's ready to go. Over time it'll become the familiar shade of charcoal black and get better with every use.

Cleaning

Never ever set aside your skillet with a bunch of water or soap to soak off the bits of food inside. That is, unless you're just plain lazy and you like watching things rust. Get the water scalding hot out of the faucet just as you're done cooking and the pan is still hot and rinse that pan clean. A soft nonmetal brush will usually do the trick, and no more than a drop or two of soap, but that's only if absolutely necessary. Next up, wipe the pan dry and rub a thin slick of cooking oil over the surface before storing. (Mine is used so often it's assigned its own burner on top of the stove.)

Eating Out and Travel: A Gluten-Free Survivor's Guide

I was surprised when someone asked me the other day, "Do you think waiters get aggravated with you?" And I said, "Why? Why would somebody get more aggravated with me, a customer with a serious health problem, than with someone who sends a sweet tea back just because it's missing a slice of lemon?" When I eat out, I tell my waiter I have a severe food allergy, and though it might sound crazy, this is the way I need you to make my food. You know what? They're cool as a cucumber with it. People in general are becoming more aware of how serious food allergies really are, such as nut allergies in kids. I find allergies most scary in children, who can't tell you what they need. If somebody gets aggravated with me because I have a food allergy, then you can be sure he'll want to change his job when I'm done with him.

On the other hand, I've had a lot of people be real curious with me and ask, "What's gluten?" Most people don't know what it is. Sometimes I swear I get flabbergasted, thinking, *You work in a restaurant and don't know what gluten is?* Which isn't good. It's a problem. That's why I look people square in the eye and say, "You cannot have these things touch my food." It is a scary feeling to be out of control in your own body and not be able to quickly fix it. If you look up a picture of me feeling helpless—or anyone, for that matter—I guarantee it won't be pretty. You just pray to God that it's going to be okay. I don't ever want to have those colossal pains and night sweats again.

Some people are more sensitive to food allergies than others. But I firmly believe no matter where you fall on that scale, if eating gluten or whatever else makes you feel like someone hooked your stomach up to a tire pump, then just don't eat it! Now I never eat at fast-food restaurants. I just can't. KFC or McDonald's? You will never ever find me there unless it's to get a Happy Meal for one of my kids. There's one place I do go to that is sort of fast food, and that's Moe's Southwest Grill. You can go into Moe's and get a bowl of rice, black beans, and grilled chicken, and they have it all right there and it's done to order. I go to my hometown Moe's a lot. They know I have an allergy, so they go out of their way to make me feel safe and sound. Trust me when I say they accommodate me. It helps to be a regular.

Other possible options are Chinese and Japanese restaurants. Chinese is often safe because they use cornstarch instead of wheat flour in their cooking. And Japanese cooking is generally rice based. Just be sure you've identified the gluten-free soy sauce. (Yes, even soy sauce usually has gluten!) I'm such a fan of Japanese grilling that my local Japanese hibachi place knows me by my first name. In fact, in my new house I'm putting in a hibachi grill!

Applebee's has a gluten-free menu, and thankfully, a lot of the other franchise restaurants are coming out with them. But if items are not called out on a menu as being specifically gluten-free, I tell people this:

1. Get simply grilled meat, like chicken or steak.

2. Order steamed broccoli or steamed mixed vegetables. You can't go wrong, and you can get that just about anywhere.

3. Good old plain rice (a Carolina standby, after all) is usually a safe bet.

4. You might think having a salad would be your best go-to option, but that's just not the case. I say stay away. What is the first thing people top a salad with? Croutons! And don't get me started on the dressing issue. Many salad dressings, even simple Italian dressings, are not gluten-free; believe me when I tell you they can be full of wheat.

5. Avoid fried food overall when you eat out because you just can't be sure it's not contaminated. Unless I am at home doing my own fried thing, I don't eat fried foods.

6. As for dessert, if the restaurant has fruit, that's great. You can always get a side of that for something sweet.

When I'm traveling I don't have time to have regular meals, so many times you'll find me with my protein shake (see page 40). But when I go to the UK, it's really tough. I love the UK, so it's hard to say this, but when we fly over there, I can never find food that's friendly to my allergies. We might have a promoter taking us around, but you don't want to be a bother to somebody. I admit that this is one of the times I do feel a little bit at a disadvantage having food allergies. So before I leave, I will spend an afternoon bagging up different snacks of things I can eat while I'm over there, and I take them along with me in my luggage. Never mind the weird looks I get from the security checkers. Water off a duck's back.

Ready to roll? If your mouth isn't watering yet, feast your eyes on these photos. When food looks this good, nobody will be asking where the gluten is! Then wipe that drool off your face, throw on an apron, and meet me in the kitchen. Time to get cookin'.

Kiss My Grits, page 42

Lemon Poppy Seed Friendship Muffins, page 44

Baking Powder Biscuits, page 50

Apple Something Fritters, page 47

Repo Ron's Kuntry Omelet, page 56

Donna D's Honey'd Oat Bread, page 58

Cheesy Bacon 'n' Corn Skillet Cakes, page 57

Flatbed's Flattering Peanut Butter and Jelly French Toast, page 62

Lizard Lick McMuffins, page 63

Nana's No-Nut Banana Bread, page 66

Every-Time Chicken Salad, page 77

Corn Casserole, page 78

Freestylin' Tacos, page 81

Alex's Simple Chicken Pie, page 80

Cold Macaroni Salad, page 84

Crawfish Salad Done Right, page 89

Hush-up Spicy Hush Puppies, page 92

Over-the-Sink BLT, page 91

Jessie-Mae's Meatball Po' Boys, page 94

Healthy Rice Salad, page 96

DJ Silver's Spicy Fried Pickles, page 106

Fancy Nancy's Crab Dip, page 110

Frozen Fruit Salad, page 116

Cookie Soup, page 117

Late-Night Twinkies, page 118

Puredee Pretzel Bites, page 120

Quick Nachos, page 122

Tuna Melt, page 128

Broccoli Cheese Dip, page 129

Old-Timey Celery Soup, page 139

Alexa's Best Ever Meatloaf, page 140

Twice-Baked Spam-tatoes, page 141

Gluten-Free Hamburger Helper, page 149

Amy's Chex Crunchy Chicken Tenders, page 151

The Shirley Steamer, page 152

Jalapeño Shrimp and Cilantro Rice, page 154

Crispy Corncob Corn Bread, page 156

Spoon Bread, page 160

Cheddar Chicken and Rice Casserole, page 145

Peanut Butter Pie, page 174

Cherries Jubilee, page 175

Gluten-Free Butterscotch Crimpets, page 177

Honey Dew Cookies, page 178

Lizard Limelight Atlantic Beach Pie, page 180

Mississippi Mud Bars, page 184

Peachy Keen Slump, page 188

Orange Upside-Down Picnic Cake, page 186

Sun Tea Cake, page 192

The 1-2-3-4 Cake, page 195

CAROLINA BREAKFASTS

When I think of the beginning of the day first I think of coffee, then I think, *Well, what the heck am I gonna eat today?* On days when we are busy filming episodes of *Lizard Lick Towing*, I'll just have one of my protein shakes (page 40) and make sure the kids are fed before we all run like stallions out the door. For me, the special breakfast times are on the weekends, when everyone is home and I can get all domestic without having to put on makeup or change my clothes.

I just love it when we are all hanging out in our pj's making Seven-Up Biscuits (page 68) or Flatbed's Flattering Peanut Butter and Jelly French Toast (page 62). For me, writing this book is like inviting you into my kitchen, my absolute favorite room in our house. So inviting you into the heart of my home is like reading the Book of Revelation—pretty major.

> **First we eat, then we do everything else.**
> • • • • •
> **—M. F. K. Fisher**

Don't worry, I ain't gonna be swatting your knuckles with a ruler, but I am gonna show you how simple and easy living like a gluten-free country-fried can be. I'm gonna make the recipes I've made my whole life, but gluten-free. Be sure to dog-ear page 26 so you don't forget the thing that makes this cookbook tick, and that is my gluten-free mix. Without the mix, you won't be able to make any of my biscuits, cakes, or cookies, and that would be a shame if you ask me, because you know what? They are better than a fresh loaf of Wonder Bread.

When I first went gluten-free, I would wake up dreading the walk downstairs to make breakfast, because I didn't know what the heck I was doing. Now I have a bounce in my step because I know that I can make anything I can think of gluten-free. And so can you!

So turn that frown upside down, pull your apron on, and smile, because we are about to have some gluten-free fun.

Carolina

BREAKFASTS

Amy's Protein Shake

When I'm training for my next power-lifting competition or when I just want to have a super-powered breakfast, I whip up one of these for the kids and me. I like this shake with a ripe banana or a green banana, so you don't have to sit around watching that banana get spots. You can make yourself one of these shakes no matter what state your bananas are in. In fact, here's a trick you can take to the bank: peel and freeze your bananas when they are just the way you like them so you can have them your way, right away. This recipe works great as a base for variations. Throw in some powdered chocolate, berries, or even shredded coconut in separate batches and you'll have something to tickle everybody's taste buds.

Makes 1 shake

2 scoops vanilla whey protein

1 handful of ice

1 ripe banana

1 teaspoon vanilla extract

1 cup cold almond milk
or regular milk

Throw everything in a blender and mix until it looks thick and smooth.

NOTES:

_____

_____

_____

_____

_____

**Courage is like a muscle.
We strengthen it by use.**

— *Ruth Gordon*

POWER LIFTING

I was a power lifter—and if you don't know what that is, I'll tell you I was strong, not beautiful, because I could lift the world—not stand and pose in it. When you're a power lifter, you can pretty much eat anything that you want to until you get ready to cut weight. But the next phase is pretty much the same kind of diet as when I'm eating gluten-free. You sub in a lot of protein, and it's actually better for you to lose the gluten in the process. It's a little hard when you power lift because you need a certain amount of sugar from carbs to give you the energy you need to work out, but it's not going to inhibit you too much when you train. In fact it might make you look more like a body builder because the diet will cut you more. Trainers will try to get you to eat at least eight times a day, and three of those are protein shakes. So in the end it's better to take the gluten out; just watch your fatigue when you are on lower carbs. Plus, more professional athletes are going gluten-free because the grains used in gluten-free don't cause lactic acid to build up in your muscles. So after a hard day of training, you won't be sore. Which is, let me tell you, amazing!

Kiss My Grits

Whenever someone tells me they don't like something, I just tell them they can kiss my grits. In case you were wondering, this recipe is what I'm thinking about when I say it. You can put your money where your mouth is, because once these grits hit the ol' pucker-upper, the boys will be lining up to kiss the cook. I like to serve this ladled hot right out of the pot, but if you find yourself with extra or needing to cook them way ahead of time, they set up nicely spread out in a casserole and chilled. Just slice and reheat and you've got a southern comfort polenta-style side dish.

Serves 4 to 6

4 slices thick slab bacon, fried until crisp, then chopped

4¼ cups water

1 cup quick grits

¼ teaspoon salt

¾ cup shredded Cheddar cheese

2 tablespoons unsalted butter

1 green onion, green parts only, sliced thin (optional)

¼ teaspoon paprika (optional)

First, fry up the bacon as you please. I really like my bacon to be crispy but a little chewy for my grits so it has that real southern feel when you take that first bite, but you know how weird people get when you start talking about bacon. I mean, really y'all, it can start a fight if you aren't careful. Anyhow, let's get back to making those grits.

Now that your bacon is done, boil the water in a big pot with the butter. When the water boils, add the grits and stir with a long-handled spoon. I don't know if you have ever gotten burned by grits jumping out of the pan, but let me tell you, it doesn't feel good, so be careful.

When the grits get good and thick, add the salt, cheese, and bacon, and the green onions and paprika if you are using 'em.

Serve right away with either a poached or a fried egg. I like fried eggs on my grits, but just like with bacon, everyone is a critic.

These grits will keep just fine in an airtight container for up to a week.

NOTES:

_____

_____

_____

Carolina Sausage Scramble

I love me some sausage and eggs first thing in the morning, and so do all my kids. Put them together with some mozzarella and you have the perfect way to start the day. Did I mention this is just about as easy a breakfast to make as they come? From start to finish, you can have this on the table in less than 20 minutes. Sometimes I throw in some chopped bell pepper or use Cheddar instead of mozzarella. And on a lazy morning an even quicker version is to use chopped-up leftover ham in place of sausage.

Serves 4

1 tablespoon unsalted butter

½ onion, diced

1 jalapeño, seeded and diced

4 breakfast sausage links, removed from the casing

6 large eggs, beaten

½ cup shredded mozzarella cheese (optional)

Melt the butter in a skillet and cook the onion with the jalapeño until the onion is translucent. Remove from the pan. Add the sausage and cook until brown.

Drain any extra grease, add the eggs, stirring with a fork, but only until they set.

Place the eggs into a bowl, top with the mozzarella cheese, if using, and serve with a spoon.

NOTES:

Lemon Poppy Seed Friendship Muffins

Make a friend for life and don't worry about the poppy seeds; this muffin is drug-free. (No kuntry additives here!) This recipe featured strong in my original list of must-have gluten-free recipes because here in the Carolina Mountains, this is considered *the* thing to serve when you have houseguests over. It doesn't matter if you've known them for years or if they are just coming into your life. You've always gotta have lemon poppy seed muffins around. Good thing these stay so moist for so long!

Makes 12 muffins

1 cup sugar

6 tablespoons unsalted butter

3 large eggs

2 cups Amy's Gluten-Free Mix

1 teaspoon baking soda

¼ teaspoon salt

3 tablespoons lemon juice

½ cup milk

1 teaspoon vanilla extract

Zest of 1 large lemon

2 tablespoons poppy seeds

Preheat your oven to 350°F. Line a 12-cup muffin tin with some paper liners. Set aside.

In the large bowl of a stand-up mixer with the paddle attachment or a handheld mixer with beaters, cream together the sugar and the butter until the mixture looks pale and fluffy. Add the eggs one at a time, then continue beating until light and fluffy.

In another bowl, mix together the gluten-free mix, baking soda, and salt, and then add that to the butter mixture. Turn the mixer off, then add the lemon juice, milk, and vanilla extract. Mix until you can no longer see any dry ingredients. Add the lemon zest and poppy seeds, and mix just until it's really in there, like 30 seconds.

Divide the batter between the cups as evenly as your eyes will allow.

Bake for 20 minutes, or until a toothpick comes out clean.

Muffins will keep in a muffin tin for up to four days.

The Mixer Mix-up: You don't have to tell me twice how frustrating it is not having the right equipment in the kitchen. So let me tell you right here, if you don't have a stand-up mixer, your handheld mixer will do just fine. And if you're relying on good old elbow grease, just let the butter soften for a few minutes before you get going on a recipe.

NOTES:

_____

_____

_____

_____

_____

_____

Countless Coconut Coffee Cake

If the morning is starting off slow, just cut off a piece of Countless Coconut Coffee Cake. It sure will give your day a jump start for countless hours of hard work. If you are sensitive to sugar, try using coconut palm sugar in place of the light brown sugar for a healthier alternative. Try bringing this to the office break room and watch them all perk up. Then tell them it's gluten-free and really knock their socks off.

Serves 8 to 10

Unsalted butter for greasing pan

1 stick unsalted butter

1 cup firmly packed light brown sugar (or coconut palm sugar)

4 large eggs

2½ cups Amy's Gluten-Free Mix

2½ teaspoons baking powder

1 teaspoon salt

1¼ cups sour cream

1 tablespoon vanilla extract

1⅔ cups shredded coconut (sweetened is best, but unsweetened is good, too)

So to get started, preheat your oven to 350°F. Rub a little butter over the bottom and sides of an 8-inch square baking pan, and set that aside.

In the large bowl of a stand-up mixer with the paddle attachment, cream together the butter and the light brown sugar (or the coconut palm sugar) until light. Add the eggs and beat on high until the mixture is fluffy. Turn the mixer off, then add the gluten-free mix, baking powder, and salt. Slowly mix in the dry ingredients, and just when you can't see them anymore, add the sour cream and vanilla extract and mix until combined.

Remove the bowl from the mixer. Using a wooden spoon, fold in the coconut.

The batter should be pretty thick. Pour it into your prepared pan, and bake for 30 to 35 minutes, or until a toothpick poked into the middle comes out clean.

Miraculously, this coffee cake keeps on the counter wrapped in plastic for a week.

Now that is what I call a gift that just keeps on giving.

NOTES:

_____

_____

_____

Apple Something Fritters

These taste so good they will make your tongue drill a hole in the top of your mouth and slap your brain around. At least that is how Ronnie describes these fritters. Mouth-watering fritters is what I call 'em when I'm not calling them by their real name. As a breakfast treat, these have got New Orleans's fancy fried dough beignets beat by a mile in my book. In fact, if you want beignets, leave out the apples and serve with an avalanche of powdered sugar.

Makes 12 fritters

FOR THE APPLES

½ cup firmly packed light brown sugar

Pinch of salt

2 tablespoons cornstarch

1 teaspoon ground cinnamon

1 apple, peeled, cored, and sliced thin

1 teaspoon vanilla extract

FOR THE BATTER

1 cup Amy's Gluten-Free Mix

½ teaspoon salt

3 tablespoons sugar

3 large eggs, separated

½ cup water

2 cups vegetable oil for frying

½ cup sugar for coating

In a medium-sized bowl, mix together the light brown sugar, pinch of salt, cornstarch, and cinnamon. Toss with your hands until the mixture forms even crumbs. Add the apple slices and the vanilla extract, and toss until evenly covered. Seal the bowl with plastic wrap and then place in the fridge for at least 1 hour.

For the batter, in a large bowl, stir together the gluten-free mix, salt, and 2 tablespoons of the sugar. Add the egg yolks and the water, and stir until thick and smooth.

Whip the egg whites on high with your handheld mixer with a pinch of salt and the remaining tablespoon of sugar. Whip those babies until they are glossy and thick.

Fold the egg whites into the batter. Heat the oil to 350°F. (See page 49 for tips on frying.) Now this next part might be a little messy, but hey, that's what soap and water are for, right?

Pour the last ½ cup sugar onto a plate and give it a shake so the sugar is flat.

Take an apple slice and dip it into the batter. Using a large metal spoon, dip the fritter into the oil and fry until golden, 1 to 2 minutes per side.

(continued)

Remove the fritter from the oil with a spoon with holes in it, and place it on a brown paper bag to drain for a minute. Then roll the fritter in the sugar and serve.

Repeat until all of your apples are fried up. They most definitely taste the best when they are hot, but that's fine because people will be grabbin' them off the plate as fast as you can cook them.

Fritters are best for only a couple of days. Reheat in the microwave for 15 seconds, then serve.

I always have apple slices left over, but that just means your vanilla ice cream just got more interesting.

NOTES:

_____

_____

_____

_____

_____

_____

FOR DEEP FRYING

Frying is so common in North Carolina that some people invest in countertop deep fryers. But there's no need for those things crowding out your toaster and Cadillac mixer. Here's the nitty-gritty on what you need to know.

1. Get a large heavy-bottomed pot, like a Dutch oven or a big canning pot, if you're deep frying. For more shallow frying, your cast-iron skillet will do.

2. A deep fry or candy thermometer is a real help to get an accurate read on the temperature of the oil. This isn't being fancy; it's just keepin' you from burning your food. But if you don't have one of those handy, you can always do the drop test. Test the heat of the oil by dropping in a little bit of batter. If it sinks, you're not hot enough, and if it quickly burns black, lower the heat. If it floats up and gently sizzles golden, you're good to go. If you're not using wet batter, stick a corner of whatever it is you're frying into the oil to test it. It should sizzle up and brown it gently.

3. Be careful with that hot oil when sliding your food in and never ever over-crowd the pot. If you do, the temperature of the oil will plummet and leave you with a mess resembling a wet washcloth.

4. If you can't tell if it's done by sight, then for heaven's sake go ahead and pull one out, crack it open and test it. There's no excuse for serving raw meat or dough, and the secret's out anyway that in fact no, you don't have X-ray vision. Plus, I love to be the tester for whatever comes out of hot oil!

Baking Powder Biscuits

Biscuits are a staple in our house just as they are all over the South. They better be flaky and good because everybody, and I mean every soul in my house, will complain if they're not up to snuff. This was one of the things I worried about when I started making them gluten-free. I mean, if you've ever tried to make a southern biscuit using northern flour, then you know what I mean. The flour needs to be tender to get the consistency right. Lo and behold, these pass the sniff and taste test with my crowd. If you keep on reading, you'll see that I use these biscuits to make all kinds of things, like my Bone Daddy Biscuits 'n' Gravy (page 52) and the Lizard Lick McMuffins (page 63). But seeing how we are from the South, you can serve these biscuits any time of day. (Just not the next day after you've left them out all night.) Pull these hot out of the oven and slap some butter, honey, strawberry jam, or heck, even some molasses on these for an easy rise 'n' shine.

Serves 6

Unsalted butter
for greasing pan

2 cups Amy's Gluten-Free Mix

1 tablespoon baking powder

2 tablespoons sugar

½ teaspoon salt

¼ cup vegetable shortening

1 cup milk

Preheat the oven to 425°F. Grease a 9-inch round cake pan with butter.

In a large bowl, combine all the dry ingredients, then add the shortening. Using the tips of your fingers, roll the shortening with the flour until the mixture looks like damp sugar. Add the milk, and mix until nice and thick. Let the dough sit for 10 minutes before rolling it out.

Dust a counter with some more mix, and roll out the dough until it's 1 inch thick. Use the top of a drinking glass or a biscuit cutter to cut out the biscuits. Place them in the cake pan. I like to get my biscuits right up next to each other so they get nice and cozy.

Bake for 10 to 15 minutes, until the biscuits are golden brown.

Eat 'em while they are hot with some butter or some Bone Daddy Gravy (page 52).

Gluten-free or not, biscuits are always best the day they are made, but if by some miracle you have some left over, throw them in a resealable bag until you're ready to eat them.

NOTES:

_____

_____

_____

_____

_____

_____

Bone Daddy Biscuits 'n' Gravy

Ronnie is my number one bone daddy, but boy, if these biscuits and gravy don't come really close to being my real number one. Even though Ronnie himself isn't gluten-free, he sure does love it when I make these for him and the kids. The trick here? Cook those onions down as much as you can stand it, because they are the ones that add the most flavor to the gravy.

Serves 6

6 Baking Powder Biscuits (page 50)

BONE DADDY GRAVY

1 whole roasted chicken

6 cups store-bought chicken stock

2 celery stalks

1 carrot

2 onions

1 bay leaf

1 teaspoon whole black peppercorns

1 teaspoon salt

2 tablespoons unsalted butter

2 tablespoons cornstarch

1 cup heavy cream

Salt and pepper to taste

Remove all the meat from the bones of the roasted chicken; reserve the cooked meat for my Every-Time Chicken Salad (page 77). I like to use store-bought roasted chickens to save time.

Put those bones into a large stockpot, and cover with the chicken stock. Add the celery stalks with the leaves on because that is where the flavor is, y'all. Peel the carrot, cut it up into 3 pieces, and throw them in. Peel and slice one of the onions in half, and add that to the stockpot, too. Throw in the bay leaf and any other fresh herbs you have lyin' around, like parsley. If you have some whole black peppercorns, those won't hurt. Add 1 teaspoon of salt.

Bring to a boil, then reduce the temperature to a simmer and cook for 1 hour.

Remove from the heat and strain the stock into a large bowl. Put 1 cup of the stock into a small pan and bring it to a boil. Reserve the rest of the stock for some soup. I like to freeze mine. Reduce the cup of stock down to ½ cup.

While the stock is cooking down, take that other onion and chop it up fine. Melt 1 tablespoon of butter in your skillet, and sauté until the onions are light brown, about 15 minutes. Pour a few tablespoons of the stock into a bowl and then whisk in the cornstarch. Pour this back into the hot stock, and whisk until it starts to get thick. Add the remaining tablespoon of butter, the cooked onions, and the cream, and then season to taste with the salt and pepper. Continue to whisk until you get the consistency you are looking for.

Ladle over your biscuits! Yum.

NOTES:

_____

_____

_____

_____

_____

_____

The Chief's Cake-Style Donuts

These are good and good for you because I bake these donuts instead of frying them. Don't worry, though; my Apple Something Fritters (page 47) will satisfy that craving—and you can even add the glaze here to those fritters if you really want to be naughty. In the meantime, these will give Dunkin' Donuts a run for their money! Just don't be callin' me if the cops start showing up for their morning fix. It's tough being so good.

Makes 12 donuts

Unsalted butter for greasing pans

3 large eggs

1 cup sugar

3 cups Amy's Gluten-Free Mix

4 teaspoons baking powder

1 teaspoon salt

1 teaspoon ground nutmeg

½ teaspoon ground cinnamon

¼ teaspoon cardamom

2 tablespoons melted unsalted butter

1 cup coconut milk or regular milk

3 teaspoons vanilla extract

Quick Glaze (opposite page)

Preheat the oven to 350°F. Grease a donut pan with butter, and set aside.

In a large bowl, mix the eggs and sugar together until light and fluffy. In another bowl, whisk together the gluten-free mix, baking powder, salt, nutmeg, cinnamon, and cardamom. Stir the dry ingredients into the eggs and sugar. Add the melted butter, milk, and vanilla extract. Mix until thick. Divide the batter into the molds in your donut pan.

Bake for 20 to 25 minutes, until the donuts are risen and slightly golden.

Cool in the pan for 10 minutes. Invert onto a wire rack to cool completely.

Make the Quick Glaze. Dunk one side of each donut in the Quick Glaze, and then return it to the wire rack so the icing can set. The icing will drip, so set a cookie sheet under the rack.

Store in an airtight container for up to three days.

NOTES:

_____

_____

_____

Quick Glaze

1 tablespoon unsalted butter

1 cup confectioners' sugar

1 teaspoon vanilla extract

1½ tablespoons milk or water

In a mixer or a large bowl, mix the butter with the sugar until you can no longer see the lumps of butter. Add the vanilla and the milk or water (if that is how you roll). Mix until very smooth. If the icing is still too thick, add ½ tablespoon more milk until it's liquid enough to pour.

NOTES:

_____

_____

_____

_____

_____

_____

Repo Ron's Kuntry Omelet

My husband loves a good omelet, but not as much as he loves me (at least that's what he says when he's sleepy). If it wasn't for the fact that he gets flustered at the prospect of a can opener crossing his path, well, I might second-guess him. It's hard when you're with a man with a demanding mono-ab, but I know this meaty omelet delivers. If you've never had an omelet with beef bologna, don't second-guess it, you're in for somethin' good. It sears up nicely and complements those red hots. (*Red hots* is redneck for hot sauce.)

Serves 2

3 large eggs

Vegetable oil or grape seed oil for pan

2 slices beef bologna, diced

3 mushrooms (I use white mushrooms), sliced

2 links red hot sausages (see my resources—it's a Carolina thing)

½ cup shredded Cheddar cheese

Salt and pepper to taste

Tabasco sauce, for serving

Crack the eggs into a medium-sized bowl, and whisk until you can no longer see the egg whites separate from the yolks.

Next, put a little oil in a skillet and get it hot. Add the diced bologna and fry it until the meat just takes on some color. Remove from the pan. In the same skillet, add the mushrooms and sauté until they get nice and limp. Remove the mushrooms from the pan, and then pour in the eggs and tilt the pan, so the eggs cover the bottom.

Using a spatula, scoot the eggs into the center of the pan, and allow the runny eggs to fill the empty spaces. When the eggs are almost totally set, put the bologna, mushrooms, sausages, and cheese on one side of the eggs. Season with salt and pepper. Fold the omelet over and turn off the heat. Leave the omelet in the pan to allow the cheese to keep melting.

Serve right away with some Tabasco sauce. *Good morning!*

The omelet will keep in the fridge for a couple of days.

NOTES:

Cheesy Bacon 'n' Corn Skillet Cakes

Throw these skillet cakes together and they will for sure say *puredee good!* I don't eat regular bacon often, but when I do, I always throw it into these skillet corn cakes and, as you've already seen, Kiss My Grits (page 42). I love skillet cakes like these because they're even quicker than quick corn bread but just as nice to eat on a cool Carolina morning. I'm not one to stand on a soapbox, but I'm going to here: if nothing else, make sure you get yourself a cast-iron skillet (see pages 28 and 29 for tips). Seasoned right, it's naturally nonstick, and not only does it fry up the best bacon of your life, you can use that bacon grease to fry up these corn cakes. When I'm feeling really fancy, I serve these with sour cream and green onions, but most of the time I like a soft-cooked egg served up on top of each crispy cake, so that the warm yolk can run into each bite.

Makes breakfast for 4

½ cup plus 1 tablespoon Amy's Gluten-Free Mix

¼ cup coarse cornmeal

¼ cup masa harina

1 teaspoon baking powder

½ teaspoon baking soda

½ teaspoon salt

2 tablespoons sugar

⅔ cup milk

2 large eggs

2½ tablespoons bacon grease, plus additional for greasing skillet

3 strips of bacon, cooked and chopped

½ cup corn kernels

⅔ cup shredded Monterey Jack cheese

In a good-sized mixing bowl, add the gluten-free mix, cornmeal, masa harina, baking powder, baking soda, salt, and sugar, and mix them up good. Next add the milk, eggs, and bacon grease. Stir until the batter thickens. Add the bacon, corn, and cheese last so they don't get in the way.

Heat up a skillet, and add a little bacon grease. Fry up the griddle cakes to any size you please. I like to make them no bigger than a duck egg because that's about how big a soft-cooked egg gets when all's said and done. And you and I both know when the vehicle gets too big for the passenger, you've got problems.

These cakes keep in an airtight container for up to a week. I suggest reheating these in the microwave before enjoying them a second time.

NOTES:

Donna D's Honey'd Oat Bread

Yes, making bread does take a smidge more of your time, but it's *well* worth setting aside a couple hours to pull together this amazing loaf. Fact is, most of the time is spent waiting for it to rise anyway, so it's not as bad as it sounds. Make a couple batches so you can freeze a loaf for later (wrap it in plastic, then a freezer-safe bag, to avoid freezer burn), then use this bread to make my Over-the-Sink BLT (page 91), Flatbed's Flattering Peanut Butter and Jelly French Toast (page 62), and anything else you can think of that needs bread. You can call me crazy when I say life just isn't the same without a good sandwich, but after you eat this gluten-free bread, you'll be saying, she might be crazy, but she sure ain't stupid!

So you're probably asking, "Okay, smarty-pants, how do I thaw that second loaf I made and froze?" Don't run for the microwave. Remove the plastic wrap and plastic bag from the loaf, then carefully rewrap the bread in a single layer of foil. Preheat the oven to 250°F, and let it reheat in there for 20 minutes. The crust will be crusty and the inside moist.

Makes 1 loaf

Unsalted butter for greasing pan

2¾ cups Amy's Gluten-Free Mix

1½ cups gluten-free quick-cooking oats

1 tablespoon yeast

½ cup milk

2 tablespoons unsalted butter

¾ cup water

3 tablespoons honey

2 large eggs

2 teaspoons salt

Glutinous rice flour or additional gluten-free mix for dusting work surface

Preheat the oven to 350°F. Grease a bread pan with unsalted butter and set aside.

In the large bowl of a stand-up mixer with a paddle attachment, add the gluten-free mix, the oats, and the yeast. Scald the milk on the stove with the butter. Add the water, honey, and eggs to the dry ingredients, and mix on high until the mixture starts to get thick. Add the warm milk, and mix on high for 2 minutes. Then add the salt, and mix on high for another 3 minutes.

Lightly dust the counter with glutinous rice flour or more gluten-free mix, and knead the dough until smooth. Shape the dough into a large pill shape and then put it in the pan. Cover the pan with plastic wrap and refrigerate for 1 hour.

Remove from the fridge, remove the plastic wrap, and drape a kitchen towel over the bread pan. Allow to rise in a warm part of your kitchen for 30 minutes. Cover with foil and bake for 25 minutes. Remove the foil and bake for 20 minutes more, until the bread is golden brown and has started pulling away from the sides of the pan.

Allow to cool for a little while before slicing. Trust me, you wanna wait. The steam can and will burn your hot little hands.

This bread keeps good for 1 week wrapped up tight in plastic wrap.

NOTES:

_____

_____

_____

_____

_____

_____

Big as Your Face Buttermilk Pancakes

I like a nice big pancake that fills up my whole plate, and these do just that and puff up like you wouldn't believe. Reminds me of IHOP on a good day when there aren't too many truckers in there. What's better than having good pancakes at home in your pj's? To make a pig in a blanket, roll these around a grilled sausage, or if you want to turn up the nutritional dial, toss some blueberries or ripe slices of peach onto the flapjack just before the flip.

Serves 4

1¼ cups Amy's
Gluten-Free Mix

3 tablespoons sugar

¼ teaspoon salt

1¼ teaspoons baking powder

¼ cup buttermilk

¼ cup milk

2 large eggs

2 tablespoons vegetable oil

2½ teaspoons vanilla extract

Unsalted butter for pan

In a nice big mixing bowl, combine the dry ingredients with a big ol' spoon. In another bowl, measure out your wet ingredients and mix with a fork. Pour the wet ingredients into the dry ingredients and mix with that spoon until nice and smooth. You really don't want big lumps of flour in there because the pancakes just don't rise the same if you ask me, so use the back of your spoon to break up those pesky lumps by pressing the spoon into the sides of the bowl.

Heat an 8-inch nonstick skillet. Melt a little butter in the pan, and then pour in ¼ cup of the batter. Smooth the batter out a bit so it coats the bottom of the pan. When little bubbles form all over the top of the pancake, it's ready to flip, usually 2 minutes or so. Flip that big old pancake and cook it some more until golden brown.

The key to the best pancakes is to get the pan just the right temperature. If it is too hot, you are gonna brown those cakes way too fast and have a raw center, so no matter how hungry you are, remember low and slow is your best bet.

These flapjacks keep well in the fridge for up to a week.

Breakfast Tip: You might not think about it, but if you have Sunday pancakes left over, they freeze really nicely. Just place waxed paper in between each of them and pop them into a sealable plastic bag. No need to thaw them—your magic microwave will heat those babies up right out of the freezer in no time the next time you want to indulge on a weekday.

NOTES:

_____

_____

_____

_____

_____

_____

Flatbed's Flattering Peanut Butter and Jelly French Toast

There is this restaurant in North Carolina called Flatbed's, and sweet lord of mercy, do they have the best French toast I have ever had. Maybe it's the Elvis in me, but I love mine with peanut butter and jelly. It's like taking my favorite childhood sandwich and making it better. A trick to good French toast is to do as the French do and use day-old bread. It'll soak up the creamy goodness in the batter much better and load on the flavor. You can use store-bought gluten-free bread, but it doesn't hold a candle to Donna D's Honey'd Oat Bread (page 58).

Serves 3

2 large eggs

¼ cup sugar

½ cup half-and-half or cream

1 teaspoon vanilla extract

¾ teaspoon ground cinnamon

Pinch of salt

6 slices of Donna D's Honey'd Oat Bread (page 58), or store-bought gluten-free bread

Unsalted butter for pan

½ cup peanut butter

½ cup jelly (strawberry, blueberry, or grape)

In a cake pan, whisk together the eggs and the sugar until the sugar stops scraping around. Add the half-and-half, vanilla extract, and ground cinnamon; a pinch of salt finishes this recipe off. Whisk just to combine.

Dip the bread in the egg mixture and allow to soak for 1 minute per side, longer for a more moist French toast.

Now take your cast-iron skillet and melt a tablespoon of butter in it. When the butter foams up like an ocean wave, fry up a couple of pieces of the toast, about 1½ to 2 minutes per side. If they are browning up too fast, lower the heat so they don't burn.

Transfer a couple of slices of toast to a plate, smear a little peanut butter and jelly over the top of each one, and serve.

Done, son!

If you have leftovers, you are crazy.

NOTES:

Lizard Lick McMuffins

Who needs McDonald's when you can have a homemade Mc-Anything? This morning muffin tastes anything but gluten-free and definitely gives the golden arches a run for their money. While I prefer it if we all sit round the table, this is the perfect type of grab-and-go, stick-to-your-ribs, one-handed breakfast that's just unavoidable some days. No ham or Canadian bacon? A slice of smoked turkey works well in a pinch. I just love it when I see Ronnie eating one of these in his T-shirt with his sleeves rolled up.

Serves 6

6 Baking Powder Biscuits (page 50) or Seven-Up Biscuits (page 68), cut in half

Unsalted butter for the biscuits

6 slices American cheese

6 slices warm Canadian bacon (or slices of ham)

6 fried large eggs, over easy

Take one of the biscuits and slather some butter on the bottom half.

Top with a slice of American cheese. Place in the microwave and heat for 20 seconds to set the cheese. Top with Canadian bacon, an over-easy egg, and the other half of the biscuit. Serve right away while it is warm.

Repeat until your whole family has eaten. Don't worry, there aren't ever any leftovers.

NOTES:

_____

_____

_____

_____

You only live once, but if you do it right, once is enough.

—Mae West

Banana Waffle Tower

You don't have to make a tower out of these to live like a gluten-free king, but it sure is a fun way to serve them for your family. Then, when you bring the waffles to the table, you just take a single layer off the tower for each person, so you can actually sit down with them instead of running back and forth between the kitchen and the table like a chicken with her head chopped off. In the unlikely event that you have leftovers, let them cool completely, seal them in a plastic bag with pieces of waxed paper in between each of them, and store them in the freezer. When you have a hankering, pop one of them out of the freezer and directly under the broiler or into your toaster oven and crisp them back up. Minus the waxed paper, of course! If you add a scoop of strawberry ice cream and a drizzle of good chocolate sauce, you've got dessert.

Serves 4

Unsalted butter or nonstick cooking spray for greasing waffle iron

2 cups Amy's Gluten-Free Mix

1 teaspoon baking soda

½ teaspoon salt, plus a pinch

3 tablespoons sugar

3 large eggs, separated

2 cups buttermilk

5 tablespoons unsalted butter, melted

4 ripe bananas, sliced, for serving

Syrup for serving

Unsalted butter for serving

Start by heating up that waffle iron of yours. Grease the iron with either butter or nonstick spray (you and I both know which one is easiest), so the waffles will let loose real easy.

Whisk together the gluten-free mix, baking soda, salt, and sugar. Add the egg yolks, buttermilk, and melted butter. Mix until smooth and somewhat thick. Whisk the egg whites with a pinch of salt until they get nice and fluffy, at least double in size. Stir the egg whites into the batter, and start frying up those waffles right away.

Ladle no more than ¼ cup into the iron; otherwise you will have a waffle waterfall on your hands.

Remember what they always say. Green light means go and red light means stop when using that waffle iron. And your car.

I like to put a layer of sliced bananas on the first waffle, then top with another and spread with butter. Keep doing this until all of your waffles have been stacked and served.

Like the pancakes, these keep for up to a week in the fridge, and they freeze like champions for up to a month in plastic bags with waxed paper between the waffles.

NOTES:

_____

_____

_____

_____

_____

_____

Nana's No-Nut Banana Bread

I love me some banana bread, but I really don't like it with nuts in it, so I got this one tailor-made from my Nana. The microwave is always a girl's best friend, especially when I'm busy chasing after the four wild monkeys masquerading as my kids, so I let it give me a helping hand in softening up the bananas here. Speaking of hungry little mouths, you might want to double this recipe so you have enough banana bread for a couple of days instead of a couple of hours. At least that's what Nana would always do.

Makes 1 loaf

Unsalted butter or nonstick cooking spray for pan

2 cups Amy's Gluten-Free Mix

2 teaspoons baking powder

¼ teaspoon baking soda

⅓ cup vegetable shortening or unsalted butter

1 cup granulated sugar

3 large eggs

2 large ripe bananas

1 tablespoon brown sugar

1 tablespoon vanilla extract

Preheat the oven to 350°F. Grease a 9 × 5 × 3-inch loaf pan with butter or nonstick spray and set aside.

Whisk together the gluten-free mix, baking powder, and baking soda in a bowl and set aside.

In the large bowl of a stand-up mixer, whip together the shortening or butter with the granulated sugar. Add the eggs and whip until light and fluffy.

Peel the bananas and heat them in a small microwave-safe bowl in the microwave for 30 seconds. Sprinkle the light brown sugar over the bananas, and microwave again for 15 seconds.

Remove the bananas from the microwave, and mash them up good with a fork.

Add the dry ingredients to the egg mixture, then immediately add the bananas and the vanilla extract and mix just until combined and smooth.

Pour the batter into the loaf pan, cover with foil, and bake for 35 to 40 minutes, or until golden brown. I like to remove the foil 5 minutes before I take the bread out of the oven.

Let the bread cool in the pan for 10 minutes, then invert it onto a wire rack to finish cooling. I like to eat my banana bread warm with a little peanut butter or salted butter.

The bread will keep wrapped in plastic for up to a week on the counter.

NOTES:

_____

_____

_____

_____

_____

_____

Seven-Up Biscuits

I loved making these biscuits as a little girl, and the mix I use here reminds me of my Bisquick-eatin' days. I can't tell you how much it makes me smile making these with my kids. If you haven't had these, don't be put off by the lemon-lime soda in the ingredient list. These puppies are famous throughout the South for their light and fluffy texture.

Serves 6 (because no one can have just one of these)

3 cups Amy's Gluten-Free Mix

4½ teaspoons baking powder

1¼ teaspoons salt

3 tablespoons vegetable shortening

½ cup (1 stick) frozen unsalted butter, separated

½ cup Greek yogurt

1 cup Diet 7UP

Preheat the oven to 450°F. Get out a 9-inch round cake pan or a cast-iron skillet.

In a large bowl, mix together the gluten-free mix, baking powder, and salt. Then using your fingers, work the vegetable shortening into the mix until it comes together real nice and you can't see any big lumps. Let sit for 10 minutes.

After the 10 minutes are over, take 4 tablespoons of the butter and grate it into the gluten-free mix. Knead the mix lightly with your fingertips. Add the yogurt and the Diet 7UP. Mix until it comes together.

Melt the remaining 4 tablespoons of butter in either your cake pan or the cast-iron skillet. Pour the melted butter into a heatproof container.

Using your hands, pat out 10 to 12 biscuits depending on how big you cut them (my mama and I used old cups to cut out our biscuits when we couldn't find the biscuit cutter, so our biscuits were always changing size) and then gingerly set them into the pan or the skillet. Brush the tops of the biscuits with the melted butter. Bake for 15 minutes, or until the biscuits are lightly browned.

Eat them hot with your favorite toppings or use them to make a devilishly good sandwich.

Biscuits are best served and enjoyed the day they are made.

NOTES:

_____

_____

_____

_____

_____

_____

My Morning Glory Muffins

It's always a glorious morning in my house. At least when I'm alone it is, but add these muffins and you have the makings of a perfect day. Some muffin recipes call for pineapple, which I can't have anyway, since I'm allergic, but I'd stand by my version as the best with apples, carrots, and pecans any day of the week. These are one of my favorite things to take along to church when they ask me to bring a healthy muffin, so you can see where I get the name from.

Makes 12 muffins

2 cups Amy's
Gluten-Free Mix

4 teaspoons baking powder

1 teaspoon salt

½ cup firmly packed light
brown sugar

¾ cup granulated sugar

Pinch of ground nutmeg

1 teaspoon ground cinnamon

¼ cup oil

2 large eggs

½ cup almond milk or
reduced-fat regular milk

½ cup diced apple
(preferably a sweet-flavored
apple like Fuji)

1 cup shredded carrot

⅓ cup finely chopped pecans

Preheat the oven to 375°F and then line your muffin pan with the necessary papers.

In a large bowl, mix the gluten-free mix, baking powder, salt, brown sugar, granulated sugar, nutmeg, and cinnamon together. In another bowl, measure out the oil, eggs, and milk and whisk together. Mix the two together with a wooden spoon.

Fold in the apple, carrot, and pecans.

Divide the batter evenly between the cups, and bake until the muffins are set and risen, about 25 to 30 minutes.

Will keep in an airtight container for up to a week (if they don't get eaten first!).

NOTES:

SOUTHERN
LUNCHES

For Ronnie and me, lunch during the week is particularly difficult because we are filming most of the time, but when I cook for him and the family on the weekends, I do them right all the way. From my Carolina Pimiento Cheese Sandwiches (page 74) to Jessie-Mae's Meatball Po' Boys (page 94), I cover one of the most important food groups there is: the sandwich. I don't know about you, but finding a good gluten-free bread is not easy. Everything out there is really expensive, and I swear there is one out there that smells like dirty gym socks when you toast it. That ain't right, so I made Donna D's Honey'd Oat Bread (page 58) gluten-free so you can see what it's like to eat a BLT over the sink when you have one foot out the door like we do.

> **Forget about the fast lane. If you really want to fly, just harness your power to your passion.**
>
> • • • • •
>
> *— Oprah*

For larger groups, I focused on all kinds of salads (Cold Macaroni Salad, page 84) and hot dishes like my Corn Casserole (page 78), so everyone gets back to work with a smile so big, people will ask what it was you were *really* doing on your lunch break.

Most important of all, every single one of these recipes is made for moving, so you can pack it up and bring it with you. 'Cause when I think of lunch, I think *Go!* Even the Hush-up Spicy Hush Puppies (page 92) travel well, because that is how we roll up here in Lizard Lick.

Southern

LUNCHES

Carolina Pimiento Cheese Sandwiches

Just because I don't eat cheese every day doesn't mean my whole family can't get in on the action. It's true I don't know much about caviar, but I do know that this is my form of Carolina caviar. The kids love these sandwiches, and I must say that when I get a hankering for cheese, I always find myself making up a pimiento cheese sandwich.

Serves 4

1 small sweet onion

½ cup gluten-free mayonnaise (I like Hellmann's), plus extra for spreading

2 (4-ounce) cans chopped pimientos, plus liquid

2 teaspoons gluten-free Worcestershire sauce (I like Lea & Perrins)

½ teaspoon cayenne pepper

1 teaspoon fresh dill (optional)

Tabasco sauce

16 ounces sharp Cheddar cheese (white or yellow), shredded

8 slices Donna D's Honey'd Oat Bread (page 58) or store-bought gluten-free bread

Grate the onion into a nice big bowl, then add the mayo, pimientos, Worcestershire sauce, cayenne pepper, dill (if using), and a dash of Tabasco. Stir everything together until combined well. Stir in the cheese.

Toast the gluten-free bread and then spread one side of each piece with extra mayo.

Now line up four slices of the bread, mayo side up, and then pile each piece with the pimiento cheese. Cover the cheese with the remaining slices of bread and serve. Sometimes I like to pop my sandwich in the microwave for just a few seconds to melt the cheese a little bit, but don't nuke it for too long. It will cause the bread to get too soft.

I also like to serve my pimiento cheese sandwiches ice cold, so be sure to chill the cheese mixture for a day before serving if this is the route you are taking.

If you have any leftovers, you are lucky. Just store it in an airtight container for up to a week.

Cryin' Onion Tip: Okay, is there anyone else out there that feels like they need to wear goggles when they cut or grate onions? They make my eyes run like faucets! One trick I've learned to stave off the waterworks show is to put the onion in the freezer for about 10 minutes just before slicing it up.

NOTES:

_____

_____

_____

_____

_____

_____

Barbeque Shrimp

When it comes to lunch, and when I actually have time to cook, I love whipping up these shrimp because they are just that easy. Be sure to keep the baby wipes handy, though. These shrimp sure can be messy with all that Lizard Lick barbeque sauce.

Serves 4

Salt and pepper

½ cup Repo Ron's Sweet Barbeque Sauce

1 pound shrimp, peeled and deveined

Lightly dust the shrimp with salt and pepper.

Pour the barbeque sauce into a resealable plastic bag and then add the shrimp. Shake it up good and refrigerate for 20 minutes.

Preheat the grill to hot.

Place the shrimp in a grill basket or on some foil and grill until just cooked through, about 8 to 10 minutes tops. Shrimp cook quick, so be a clock-watcher if you have to; there's nothing worse than an overcooked shrimp!

Eat right away with some Anytime Coleslaw (page 85).

NOTES:

_____

_____

_____

_____

_____

_____

Every-Time Chicken Salad

While I was growing up, my mama never let one bit of anything go to waste. She was always creating something new out of something else she made the day before to keep things interesting and make sure her trash can was less than full. Her chicken salad is one of those "something new" recipes that you will find yourself making every time you have some leftover chicken lying around. This might remind you a little of a Waldorf chicken salad, but there's no grapes or walnuts in this recipe. Instead you'll find dried cherries and almonds here, and don't you know it, it's better Mama's way.

Serves 4

2 cups chopped
cooked chicken

⅔ cup gluten-free
mayonnaise
(I like Hellmann's),
plus more to taste

1 celery rib, thinly sliced

1 green onion, just the
green bits, sliced

⅔ cup sliced almonds,
crushed

⅔ cup dried cherries
or dried cranberries

2 teaspoons chopped fresh
dill or 1 teaspoon dried dill

Salt and pepper to taste

In a large mixing bowl, add all the ingredients and mix until uniform. Cover with plastic and refrigerate for 15 minutes, then remove from the fridge and add more mayonnaise, since the chicken likes to soak it up as it cools. I add one tablespoon at a time until it gets to be the consistency I like, which is anything but dry. Since I know everyone's a critic when it comes to chicken salad, I'm not gonna start crap. I'm gonna leave the stink on the corner and let you decide how to finish it off before serving.

NOTES:

_____

_____

_____

_____

_____

_____

Corn Casserole

I like to serve this casserole for lunch, but it's also great as a side for dinner. Around these parts, it's always good to have a quick-to-prepare nice hot dish you can take to a friend's house at a moment's notice. This one always seems a good bet, no matter what we are eating. We are corn fed and country strong in Lizard Lick.

Serves 4

Salted butter or bacon fat for greasing dish

2 cups whole-kernel corn, fresh, frozen, or canned

1 small onion, diced

½ green bell pepper, diced

1 (8-ounce) can peeled and diced Roma tomatoes

1 teaspoon salt

1 teaspoon sugar

¼ teaspoon freshly ground black pepper

1 teaspoon fresh or dried parsley or cilantro

4 slices bacon, fried crisp and chopped

1 cup gluten-free cracker crumbs (I like Glutino)

Preheat the oven to 375°F. Grease a 2-quart casserole dish with either salted butter or bacon fat.

If you are using fresh corn, cut it from the cob, or defrost the frozen corn or drain the canned corn. Pour the corn into a medium-sized bowl, then add the onion, bell pepper, tomatoes, salt, sugar, black pepper, and parsley or cilantro. Mix everything together and then pour it into your greased dish.

In another bowl, mix together the crumbled bacon and the crushed cracker crumbs. Sprinkle this on top of the casserole, and bake for 25 to 30 minutes.

NOTES:

Grilled Cheddar Cheese Triangles

There really isn't anything that can beat a good grilled cheese sandwich and I love to have just a bite every now and then. I can't eat dairy very often, but when I do, these sure hit the spot when I don't have time to make my Carolina Pimiento Cheese Sandwiches (page 74). You can use dairy-free cheese here, but let's call the kettle black, shall we? A grilled cheese just ain't the same without a good sharp Cheddar cheese. You could always slip a slice of tomato or ham into one of these, but really, for me it's all about that gooey melted good stuff.

Makes 3 sandwiches

6 slices Donna D's Honey'd Oat Bread (page 58) or store-bought gluten-free bread

Whipped salted butter for bread

2 tablespoons unsalted butter for pan

12 slices sharp Cheddar cheese (I prefer Cracker Barrel)

Spread one side of each of the slices of bread with the whipped butter and set aside, butter side up.

Melt one tablespoon of the unsalted butter over medium heat in a nice big skillet so you can fit two sandwiches in there at the same time.

When the butter foams, place two slices of the bread, buttered side down, into the hot skillet, and then layer slices of the cheese onto the bread. You want this over a medium flame so the bread doesn't brown faster than the cheese is melting. When the cheese starts to melt, place the other slice of bread on top, buttered side up. Flip the sandwich and brown the other side.

Repeat to make the third sandwich. Cut into triangles and serve.

NOTES:

Alex's Simple Chicken Pie

This is by far one of the easiest pie recipes on the planets, seeing how almost everything in it comes out of a can. So get that can opener sharpened and dust up that rolling pin. It's time to get crackin' on Alex's deliciously rich chicken pie.

Serves 6

1 recipe Golden Pie Crust
(page 170)

Amy's Gluten-Free Mix
or glutinous rice flour for
dusting work surface

1 can chicken and rice
chowder (I like Progresso)

Preheat the oven to 400°F.

Remove the crust dough from the fridge and then dust your counter with my gluten-free flour mix or with some glutinous rice flour.

Roll out half of the crust dough to ¼ inch thick, and then line a 10-inch pie pan with it. Leave enough overhang so you can pinch the top layer to the bottom layer. Pour the can of chowder into the crust. Roll out the other half of the crust dough, and then lay it on top of the pie. Using your fingers, pinch the top layer to the bottom. Now, using a sharp knife, cut some vent holes in the top.

Bake for 25 to 30 minutes, or until the crust dough has browned and the pie filling is bubbling.

Allow to cool for at least 20 minutes before slicing, so the pie can hold its middle together. Or you can just spoon it out like we do when we just can't wait.

NOTES:

Freestylin' Tacos

Have you ever had Frito Pie in a Frito bag? Well, this is pretty much the same thing, just a touch more fancy, since I serve mine in a bowl. I love making these tacos for times when you just don't have time to sit down and eat a messy taco. This one is all messed up before it's time to eat, so you can just grab a spoon and be done. My daughter Maggie loves to make these.

Serves 6

1 tablespoon oil

1½ pounds ground beef

1 package gluten-free taco seasoning mix (I like McCormick)

4 cups Fritos

1 cup shredded Colby cheese

1 cup thinly sliced iceberg lettuce

¼ cup sour cream (optional)

Chopped fresh cilantro, to garnish

Heat a tablespoon of oil in a skillet, and when it's good and hot, add the ground beef and sauté until the meat is brown all over, about 10 minutes. Add the taco seasoning mix and the amount of water that's called for on the mix package.

Crush up the Fritos. Place a handful of the Fritos in the bottom of a small bowl, then spoon some of the beef over the top. Sprinkle with cheese, lettuce, a dollop of sour cream if that's your thing, and some cilantro.

Repeat until your whole family is served. I like to let the kids make these for Ronnie and me when we are just too gosh darn tired to cook.

NOTES:

_____

_____

_____

Stop wearing your wishbone where your backbone ought to be.

—Elizabeth Gilbert

Amy's Hot, I Mean Bra-Burning Hot, Wings

The flip side of having to give up some of my favorite sweets (until I began to crack the code on how to adapt them, that is) is that I've also always been a huge chicken person. I have to say my favorite dish of all time is boneless chicken rolled in a Buffalo wing sauce. But men, they like finger food. So all righty, ladies. If the way to a man's heart is through his stomach, then I suggest making these hot wings for your husband for dinner tonight. They are sure to get his attention, if you know what I mean. It never hurts to throw on a new T-shirt from Target while you're making 'em. I don't know what it is, but Ronnie can smell a new T-shirt before I even walk into the room.

Serves 3

12 chicken wings, tips of wings cut off

4 tablespoons unsalted butter

½ cup Amy's Lil' Firecracker Hot Sauce

1 teaspoon gluten-free Worcestershire sauce (I like Lea & Perrins)

3 shakes of Tabasco

Celery sticks for serving

Blue Cheese Dressing (opposite page) for serving

Preheat the grill to medium-high heat.

Place the wings on the grill and close the lid. Cook, turning them every few minutes, until the meat is no longer pink, about 15 to 20 minutes. Set wings aside.

Melt the butter in a large saucepan, and toss the wings in the pan until evenly coated. In a big bowl, mix together the hot sauce with the Worcestershire and Tabasco. Toss the wings in the hot sauce and serve with celery sticks and Blue Cheese Dressing.

Wing Tip: I like to cook my wings on the grill instead of deep frying them to melt all that extra fat off. Plus, the skin gets nice and crispy. But with all that fat dripping off you have to beware of flare-ups with the flames. If that happens, don't let it get the best of you (or singe your lovely long eyelashes off). Just take care and use a long pair of grill tongs to move the wings over to a cooler side of the grill grate. If it's real bad, shut the lid and close the vents to snuff out the fire.

NOTES:

_____

_____

Blue Cheese Dressing

1½ cups blue cheese crumbles

2 teaspoons gluten-free Worcestershire sauce

¼ cup buttermilk

¼ cup gluten-free mayonnaise
(I like Hellmann's)

Mix all the ingredients together in a bowl until well combined. Serve with the hot wings or use for salad dressing.

Will keep for up to a week in the fridge.

NOTES:

_____

_____

_____

_____

_____

Cold Macaroni Salad

When we have big parties on the set of *Lizard Lick Towing* or just need something to live in the fridge long enough to keep everyone fed, I like to make a big ol' batch of this cold macaroni salad. I swear sometimes it's gone before I even finish putting the plastic wrap on the bowl. Now, like my Every-Time Chicken Salad (page 77), I like to refrigerate this for 15 to 30 minutes, then add a little more mayo to get the seasoning just right. This makes it so good, you'll be grinning like a baked bean possum!

Serves 6

1 pound gluten-free shell pasta

2 celery ribs, diced

½ cup diced red bell pepper

½ cup diced green bell pepper

1 large carrot, peeled and grated

½ teaspoon dry mustard

½ teaspoon white pepper

¼ teaspoon cayenne pepper

1 cup gluten-free mayonnaise (I like Hellmann's)

2 teaspoons dill weed

Salt and ground black pepper to taste

Boil the pasta until it is tender, and then drain and rinse it so the shells don't stick to one another.

Add the celery, bell pepper, carrot, dry mustard, white pepper, cayenne pepper, mayonnaise, and dill weed, and stir well. Season to taste with salt and pepper.

Cover and refrigerate until ready to serve.

I like to add a little extra mayo right before I serve so everything is shining.

NOTES:

Anytime Coleslaw

The name of this recipe pretty much says it all. It's so good, you can enjoy it any old time you please. In the summertime, I like to throw in some peaches for a little sweet zing.

Serves 6

1 cup gluten-free mayonnaise (I like Hellmann's)

3 tablespoons apple cider vinegar

2 tablespoons sugar

1 teaspoon salt

1 cabbage, 2 to 3 pounds

½ cup shredded carrots

2 tablespoons chopped green onions

1 teaspoon celery seed

1 teaspoon dill seed

4 strips bacon, crumbled

1 to 2 ripe peaches, peeled and diced (optional)

Salt and freshly ground pepper to taste

In a medium-sized mixing bowl, whisk together the mayonnaise, apple cider vinegar, sugar, and salt until very smooth.

Shred the cabbage in the food processor until it's all the same size. Transfer the shredded cabbage into a large bowl. Add the carrots, green onions, celery seed, dill seed, crumbled bacon, and peaches, if desired. Toss with your hands to mix well.

Pour the dressing around the edge of the bowl, and toss the cabbage with your hands until well combined. Season with additional salt and some freshly ground black pepper to taste.

Cover and refrigerate until ready to serve. The slaw will hold up well for a couple of days.

NOTES:

The Power-Lifter Grilled Chicken Salad

When I'm training for my next power-lifting competition, I like to have this salad a few days a week, it's so good. It's perfect for all you heavy-lifting mamas out there like me.

Serves 2

1 head romaine lettuce

¼ cup sunflower seeds

¼ cup turkey bacon bits

1 carrot, peeled and shredded

½ cucumber, cut in half, then into half-moons

½ cup raw broccoli florets

Gluten-free Italian dressing (store-bought is fine)

2 whole chicken breasts

1 tablespoon unsalted butter

1 tablespoon vegetable oil

Salt and pepper

2 hard-cooked large eggs, cut in half

Cut or tear the lettuce into bite-sized pieces. Transfer the lettuce into a large bowl. Add the sunflower seeds, turkey bacon bits, carrot, cucumber, and broccoli.

Drizzle the dressing around the edge of the bowl. Toss with your hands.

Split the breasts (cut them in half horizontally). Melt the butter and oil in a sauté pan. When the butter foams, place two pieces of the chicken breast into the pan. Generously salt and pepper the chicken. Cook for 2 to 3 minutes. Flip the chicken and finish cooking for another 3 minutes, being sure to season this side with a little salt and pepper while you are at it.

Repeat with the other chicken breast. When the chicken is cooked, place on a cutting board and slice.

Divide the lettuce on two serving plates. Distribute the chicken and then the hard-cooked eggs over the lettuce. Serve while the chicken is still hot!

NOTES:

HARD-COOKED EGGS

The trick to making perfect hard-cooked eggs is as simple as tying your shoe: once you do it right for the first time, you just don't forget.

For starters, you want to use old eggs. Not rotten ones, of course, but not freshly laid ones, either. One- to two-week-old eggs are the best. Second, you don't ever want to boil the water the eggs are in. All this does is throttle the eggs around and cause them to crack, making one heck of a stink. So here is what you do instead:

Place the eggs into a pot of water. Bring to a simmer, and simmer for 10 minutes.

When the buzzer blows, gently plunge the eggs into ice-cold water so the egg white will separate from the shell.

Gently crack and peel the eggs and then use them as you see fit. Keep this technique in mind when you're making my Butter-Me-Up Deviled Eggs (page 108), so your eggs don't look like they were shot out of a triple-barrel shotgun.

Crab Cakes

I'll be the first to tell you that I don't make crab cakes all that often, but that doesn't mean I don't know how to make them. Fancy, yes, but you know what they say about getting fancy, don't you? The moment you get fancy is the moment it's time to wash the truck.

Serves 6

6 tablespoons unsalted butter

1 onion, finely diced

**1 cup gluten-free
bread crumbs**

**1 teaspoon salt,
plus some for dusting**

¼ teaspoon black pepper

1 teaspoon dry mustard

3 large eggs

2 tablespoons heavy cream

**1 pound crabmeat,
thawed if frozen**

2 tablespoons parsley

½ cup Amy's Gluten-Free Mix

Melt 3 tablespoons butter in a big skillet over medium-high heat. Cook the onions until they are translucent. Dust with a little salt. Toss the bread crumbs with the teaspoon of salt, black pepper, and dry mustard. Add the bread crumbs to the onions, and mix until the bread crumbs absorb all the butter. Pour the bread crumb mixture into a large bowl. Add the eggs and heavy cream, and mix well. Add the crab and parsley, and mix until nice and thick.

Shape the mixture into crab cakes. You should get 6 big cakes. Pour the gluten-free mix onto a large dinner plate.

Melt the last 3 tablespoons of butter in a large skillet over medium-high heat.

Roll the crab cakes in the gluten-free mix to evenly coat them. Fry a couple of cakes at a time in the butter until all of your cakes are cooked and golden brown, about 5 to 6 minutes per side.

NOTES:

Crawfish Salad Done Right

Got leftover crawfish from that crawfish boil? Well, even if you don't, frozen crawfish tails work just fine for this salad, too. I hope you don't go through the trouble of setting crawfish traps just to make this, but if you do, it will taste that much better. You can omit any of the seafood you wish, but be sure to replace it with more of something else. So let's say you omit the crab claw meat—just add more shrimp!

Serves 6

½ cup crab claw meat,
bits removed

2 cups boiled crawfish tails

½ pound boiled,
peeled shrimp

2 large celery stalks, sliced
(about 1 cup)

¼ cup green bell pepper

¾ teaspoon salt

⅛ teaspoon ground
black pepper

½ cup gluten-free
mayonnaise
(I like Hellmann's)

3 tablespoons lemon juice

Pinch of cayenne pepper

Mix everything together in a bowl and then refrigerate until you are ready to serve. It's really that easy. (I like to mix the mayo and lemon juice together before stirring it into the rest of the ingredients.)

Will keep in an airtight container for up to three days before getting funky.

NOTES:

Gabe's Sky-High Burger and Fries

My son Gabe loves burgers and fries more than anything, so seeing how this is his personal favorite, I named it after him. I like to use ground beef chuck, but any old ground beef will work in a pinch. Gabe is always shooting for the sky, because there's no limit to his dreams.

Serves 4

Nonstick cooking spray

1 bag frozen gluten-free French fries

1 pound ground beef chuck

1 tablespoon gluten-free Worcestershire sauce (I like Lea & Perrins)

1 teaspoon salt

1 teaspoon black pepper

Olive oil

4 slices American or other cheese (optional)

Gluten-free hamburger buns (store-bought is fine)

Slices of red onion and tomato, pickles, lettuce, mayonnaise, ketchup, and mustard for serving

Line either a roasting pan or a cookie sheet with aluminum foil. Spray with nonstick spray, and then dump the frozen fries onto the foil. Shake and unstick any fries clumped together. Dust all the fries with a little salt, and bake according to the package instructions.

In a large bowl, mix the ground chuck with the Worcestershire sauce, salt, and pepper. Shape into 4 patties. Coat the outside of the patties with olive oil, and then dust lightly with a little extra salt and pepper.

Preheat the grill to hot.

Grill those hamburgers until they are to your liking. Just remember 3 minutes per side for rare, 4 minutes per side for medium, and 5 minutes per side for well done.

If you are making cheeseburgers, a few minutes before the burgers are done, lay a slice of cheese on top of each patty and cook just until the cheese melts. It helps to lower the lid to get a good melt on harder cheeses like Cheddar.

Store-bought gluten-free buns are best when toasted, so once they are ready to go, dress your burger up any way you please and serve them while they are hot!

NOTES:

Over-the-Sink BLT

If you've never had a BLT while standing over the kitchen sink, then you haven't ever really had one. Use the ripest tomatoes you can get your hands on so the juices really drip down your forearms and into the sink.

Serves 3

6 slices Donna D's Honey'd Oat Bread (page 58) or store-bought gluten-free bread

½ cup gluten-free mayonnaise (I like Hellmann's)

1 tomato, sliced

Salt and pepper to taste

3 slices provolone cheese

9 thick slices cooked bacon

Iceberg lettuce

Toast the bread, then slather one side of all 6 slices with mayonnaise. Add a slice of tomato, and salt and pepper it up good. Top the tomato with the cheese and then the bacon. Put a few pieces of iceberg lettuce on the bacon, and then top with another slice of bread. Stand over the sink and eat it up.

Bacon Tips: Love bacon but not too keen on that big mess it leaves on your stovetop? Try cooking it in the oven. Just place the bacon slices flat on a broiler pan (you can line it with foil for easier cleanup, but they won't get as crispy). Place the pan in a cold (not preheated) oven, and then set the temperature to 400°F. Let it alone in the oven for about 18 minutes or so, adjusting the time as needed for your crispness preference. Done and done. Of course I'm a tried-and-true cast-iron bacon-frying woman, but I've also been known to use the microwave. Just place the strips between paper towels and cook on high for about 5 minutes. You just never know when life will throw you a curve ball, so you might as well know how to make bacon in 5 minutes or less!

NOTES:

_____

_____

_____

_____

Hush-up Spicy Hush Puppies

You can make these with just the cornmeal if you're feeling less fancy, but I'll be darned if these hush puppies aren't some of the best finger foods in Carolina. This is hands down one of the most asked-for recipes when it comes to southern gluten-free foods, and this version won't disappoint all those puppy lovers.

Serves 6 (45 pups)

3 cups vegetable oil

2 cups cornmeal

1 cup Amy's Gluten-Free Mix

1 teaspoon baking powder

2 tablespoons sugar

½ cup corn kernels

1 tablespoon Cajun seasoning

1 teaspoon salt

½ teaspoon black pepper

1 (10-ounce) can chunk white chicken, shredded

¾ cup grated onion

2 cloves garlic, minced

1 small tomato, diced

2 large eggs

¾ cup milk

¼ teaspoon Tabasco sauce

Spicy Horseradish Sauce (opposite page), for serving

Preheat the oil in a deep fryer or Dutch oven to 340°F. (See page 49 for tips on frying.) Combine all the remaining ingredients, and mix until nice and thick. Being very careful so you don't burn yourself, spoon the puppies into the hot oil, and fry for 4 to 5 minutes, turning the puppies over a few times while they are frying so they are brown on all sides.

Transfer to a paper bag to drain. Serve with Spicy Horseradish Sauce.

NOTES:

_____

_____

_____

_____

_____

_____

Spicy Horseradish Sauce

**1 cup gluten-free mayonnaise
(I like Hellmann's)**

**¼ cup prepared horseradish,
drained**

Salt and pepper to taste

Combine the mayonnaise and horseradish, and mix until
uniform. Season with salt and pepper to taste. Serve with your
fresh hush puppies.

NOTES:

Jessie-Mae's Meatball Po' Boys

Absolutely everyone loves Jessie-Mae's Meatball Po' Boys, and you can always tell when Ronnie's been eatin' 'em. Just check and see if he's got red sauce all over his shirt. Good thing he always has a spare (shirt) in his truck. Our version adds a slick of spicy mustard on the buns before the cheese gets melted, for an extra bite of flavor. These meatballs are also really delicious served over spaghetti.

Serves 6

4 slices gluten-free bread

¾ cup buttermilk

¾ pound ground pork

½ pound ground beef or veal

½ cup grated Parmesan cheese

3 cloves garlic, minced

1 tablespoon fresh parsley, chopped

1 teaspoon fresh oregano, chopped

½ teaspoon onion powder

¾ teaspoon salt

½ teaspoon ground black pepper

¼ teaspoon ground nutmeg

¼ teaspoon chili powder

1 large egg

Remove the crusts from the slices of bread, then crumble the bread into crumbs and place in a bowl. Pour the buttermilk over the bread, and allow it to sit for 15 minutes.

In the meantime, combine the pork, beef or veal, Parmesan cheese, garlic, parsley, oregano, onion powder, salt, pepper, nutmeg, and chili powder. Using your hands, combine well.

Using a fork, mash the bread crumbs into a paste. Add to the meat along with the egg.

Preheat the oven to 400°F.

Roll the meat into balls of the same size. I like to eyeball it, but if you've got one of those fancy scoopers like Martha Stewart, by all means use it. When all of your meatballs have been formed, place them on a baking sheet and bake them for 20 minutes, turning the meatballs every 5 minutes.

Remove from the oven.

6 gluten-free buns

3 tablespoons spicy mustard

2 cups gluten-free pasta sauce (store-bought is fine)

2 cups shredded mozzarella cheese

Slather a bun with some mustard, add a layer of the pasta sauce, and then sprinkle with the mozzarella cheese. Melt the cheese either in the microwave or in the oven, then cover the melted cheese with a few of the meatballs.

Serve immediately.

NOTES:

_____
_____
_____
_____
_____
_____

Healthy Rice Salad

This is as healthy a salad as they come and really tasty to boot. You can add sliced almonds for an even bigger yum factor. I like to make this for all my friends on their diets.

Serves 4

2 tablespoons balsamic vinegar

1½ tablespoons oil

2 cups cooked white rice

⅓ cup chopped green onion

¼ cup chopped green bell pepper

¼ cup canned Roma tomatoes, chopped

½ cup minced celery

3 tablespoons chopped fresh parsley

Salt and pepper to taste

To make the dressing, grab an old mason jar or an old jelly jar and add the vinegar and oil. Shake it up real good.

Next, mix the rice, green onion, bell pepper, Roma tomatoes, celery, and parsley in a bowl, and season to taste with salt and pepper.

Pour the dressing over the rice, and toss with your hands. (That's what God created sinks and soap for, people.) Serve or cover and store in the refrigerator. As salt has a way of getting soaked up while the salad is in the refrigerator, reseason with salt and pepper as necessary when ready to serve.

The salad keeps great for up to a week.

Rice Tip: This salad works best with nice and firm Carolina rice. Rinse your grains before you cook the rice to get all that starch off and avoid its clumping up in the bowl.

NOTES:

_____

_____

_____

_____

_____

_____

Tuna Salad

Tuna salad is another thing that I keep in the fridge for two reasons. One, because I love it, and two, because I love it. Make that three reasons! This here salad also happens to make the best Tuna Melt (page 128) this side of the Mississippi.

Serves 6

⅓ cup gluten-free mayonnaise
(I like Hellmann's)

2 teaspoons gluten-free Worcestershire sauce
(I like Lea & Perrins)

2 teaspoons lemon juice

2 (5-ounce) cans tuna

½ cup chopped celery

2 tablespoons finely chopped green onion

1 teaspoon minced dill or parsley

Salt and pepper to taste

Lettuce and slices of gluten-free toast, for serving

In a small bowl, mix up the mayonnaise, Worcestershire sauce, and lemon juice.

Drain the tuna, flake it apart with a fork, and place it in a large bowl. Add the celery and the green onion. Stir in the dressing and then add either dill or parsley. Mix until just combined. Like the Every-Time Chicken Salad (page 77), you may need to add more mayo, depending on how you like your tuna salad. Season to taste with salt and pepper.

Serve on a bed of lettuce with some gluten-free toast.

NOTES:

_____

_____

_____

_____

_____

My Way Potato Salad

Having an opinion about potato salad is like talking politics where I come from, but no matter what you believe is the best potato salad, I know mine is the clear winner. (Heck, when it comes to food, everyone in Carolina is fit to be tied!) How's that for fighting words? Just follow the sound of my voice and you'll be on your way to spud salad glory.

Serves 6

6 medium red potatoes (2½ pounds)

1 tablespoon plus 1½ teaspoons salt

2 hard-cooked large eggs, diced

½ cup chopped celery

½ cup diced sweet pickles

¼ cup chopped onion

1 tablespoon poppy seeds

⅛ teaspoon ground black pepper

1 cup French Dressing (opposite page)

Paprika for garnish

In a medium saucepan, boil the potatoes in water with 1 tablespoon salt until they are fork tender, about 15 minutes. I like to leave the skin on, but you can remove it all the same and this salad will turn out just fine.

When the potatoes are done, drain them and rinse them in cold water so you can actually handle them without burning yourself. Dice them up, trying to make the pieces as much the same size as possible.

Add the celery, pickles, onion, poppy seeds, 1½ teaspoons salt, and black pepper. Stir in the French dressing, and then refrigerate until ready to serve.

I like my potato salad as cold as it can get. It will keep in an airtight container for up to a week.

NOTES:

_____

_____

_____

_____

_____

_____

French Dressing

1 cup gluten-free mayonnaise
(I like Hellmann's)

1 teaspoon salt

1 teaspoon dry mustard

½ teaspoon paprika

½ teaspoon sugar

¼ cup red wine vinegar

In a small bowl, stir together the mayonnaise, salt, dry mustard, paprika, sugar, and vinegar. Stir until very smooth and set aside until you are ready to use it.

NOTES:

_____

_____

_____

_____

_____

_____

APPETIZERS, NIBBLES,
AND LATE-NIGHT SNACKS

Ronnie and I love to entertain, so in this chapter, you are going to find all kinds of fun ideas for your next country-posh get-together. Ever had Devils on Horseback (page 115)? Or what about some gluten-free Spicy Fried Pickles (page 106) that even your gluten-eating friends will love? If you're wondering why there are so many recipes for different dips, that's because when you walk into a party in North Carolina, there are always at least these two things: a dip and something to deliver that dip into your mouth.

> **Without leaps of imagination, or dreaming, we lose the excitement of possibilities. Dreaming, after all, is a form of planning.**
> • • • • •
> —*Gloria Steinem*

Truth be told, when I was writing up this chapter, I wanted to have something for every time of day because our schedules are nuttier than a five-pound fruitcake, and sometimes we never know when we are gonna eat. That's what the Lick Life will do, but we don't mind. It's kind of romantic when Ronnie and I are standing in the light of the refrigerator at one in the morning trying to decide if we should have Cookie Soup (page 117) or if I should whip up some Late-Night Twinkies (page 118) before we hit the hay. And the best part is, I know that we aren't alone.

So open up your refrigerator and start dreaming. That's what this chapter is all about.

Appetizers, Nibbles,

AND LATE-NIGHT SNACKS

DJ Silver's Spicy Fried Pickles

Whenever I make this recipe, I always hum to myself "Wet, dry, dredge, fry" so I don't forget what I'm doing. You can use pretty much any shape pickle you want, but I've noticed that the ones that look like chips fry up like chips. I made this recipe for one of my best friends, DJ Silver. I've known Silver since we were both dirt on the road, and ever since I went gluten-free, he has been ribbing me that I can't make a good fried pickle, so I told him to put this on his turntable and scratch on it a bit. And guess what? Even though he's not gluten-free, he prefers my pickles to anyone else's.

Makes enough for 4 people as a starter

1 (16-ounce) jar hamburger dill chip pickles

¾ cup buttermilk

1 large egg

⅛ teaspoon Tabasco sauce (1 to 2 shakes of the bottle)

1½ cups vegetable oil for frying

1 cup Amy's Gluten-Free Mix

¼ teaspoon paprika

½ teaspoon garlic powder

½ teaspoon onion powder

⅛ teaspoon cayenne pepper (optional)

⅛ teaspoon black pepper

Drain your pickles in a colander so all the extra juices drip into the sink and not onto your counter. You kinda want the pickles to be a little dry so the batter will stick to them better.

In a small bowl, mix together the buttermilk, egg, and Tabasco sauce with a fork until it's all the same color and you can't see any more of the egg yolk.

Begin heating the oil to 360°F. (See page 49 for frying tips.)

In a separate bowl, mix together all the dry ingredients.

I like to dump 3 or 4 pickles into the buttermilk mix and then transfer them into the flour mix, being sure to coat all sides of the pickles perfectly by giving the pan a good shake.

Put the breaded pickles in the hot oil, and fry them until they are golden brown—about 2 minutes, tops.

NOTES:

A Cheese Ball

While I was growing up, there was always a cheese ball at the parties my mama would drag me to, and the funny thing was, no one ever knew what the cheese ball was called other than a cheese ball. So I stuck with tradition and left this recipe nameless. Sometimes you just gotta call it what it is—just another cheese ball.

Serves 8

1 cup finely chopped pecans

2 (8-ounce) packages cream cheese, at room temperature

2 cups grated white sharp Cheddar cheese

⅓ cup gluten-free breakfast sausage, crumbled and browned

2 teaspoons gluten-free Worcestershire sauce (I like Lea & Perrins)

2 teaspoons green onion, just the green parts, sliced thin

Gluten-free crackers for serving

Scatter the finely chopped pecans on a plate for the rolling of the cheese ball.

In a large bowl, whip the cream cheese until it is very smooth. (I hope you have a handheld mixer for this one. Even cream cheese at room temperature takes a lot of elbow grease to get smooth.) Add the grated cheese, the browned breakfast sausage, the Worcestershire sauce, and the green onion. Roll the mixture into a ball between the palms of your hands until it is nice and smooth, then roll it in the chopped pecans. Refrigerate for a couple of hours so the cheese ball can set, and then serve with gluten-free crackers.

NOTES:

_____

_____

_____

_____

_____

_____

Butter-Me-Up Deviled Eggs

Everyone thinks that fresh eggs make the best deviled eggs, and they couldn't be more wrong. Just remember, fresh eggs make the ugliest deviled eggs you've ever seen. (See my tips for hard-cooked eggs on page 87.) I like the way the salted butter tastes in the egg yolks in this recipe; it also makes them super creamy. You can use this recipe as a template to do a wide range of things. Sub in capers or minced bread and butter pickles for the olives, or add a dash of hot curry powder and a few drops of lemon juice for a little warmer spice.

Makes 24 deviled eggs

12 large eggs

2 teaspoons Dijon mustard

¼ cup minced black olives

¼ teaspoon ground black pepper

Pinch of cayenne pepper

⅓ cup gluten-free mayonnaise (I like Hellmann's)

3 tablespoons salted butter, at room temperature

Paprika for garnish

Place the eggs in a nice big pot and cover them with at least 1 inch of water. Bring to a gentle boil for 30 seconds, and then remove the pot from the heat and place a lid on it. Let the eggs sit for 10 minutes, and then place the pot in the sink and let cold water fill up the pan and wash over the eggs. Let the eggs cool completely so the egg whites will detach from the shell. Then gently tap the eggs on the counter and peel them.

Cut the eggs in half lengthwise, and gingerly remove the yolks. Place the egg white halves on a nice big plate and set aside.

In a bowl, mix the yolks, mustard, olives, black and cayenne pepper, mayonnaise, and butter until the filling comes together.

Put the filling in a resealable bag, snip off one of the corners, and squeeze the filling into the cooked egg white halves. (You can use a small spoon and still get a great-looking deviled egg.)

Arrange the eggs on a platter, sprinkle a little paprika over the top of each, and serve.

NOTES:

_____

_____

_____

_____

My Midnight Omelet

I might be training for another power-lifting competition or getting ready to film another season of *Lizard Lick Towing* or running around with my kids, but no matter what I'm doing, sometimes a girl just needs a little extra shot of protein to get her through the day. And when your day ends at midnight like mine does, well, you take what you can get. This is my favorite breakfast for dinner.

Serves 1

3 large eggs (or just the egg whites)

1 teaspoon unsalted butter

2 slices deli ham, diced

2 slices deli turkey, diced

2 slices crispy cooked bacon, diced or left whole

½ cup shredded sharp Cheddar cheese

Salt and pepper to taste

Crack the eggs into a bowl and whisk until you can no longer see the egg whites separate from the yolks. If you are using just the whites, whisk them up good so you break up the white as best you can.

Melt the butter in a skillet or frying pan over medium heat. When it foams up good, add the eggs all at once, and swirl them around in the pan so the bottom is totally covered.

Using a spatula, scoot the eggs into the center of the pan and allow the runny eggs to fill the empty spaces. Be sure to keep the flame under the pan low. If you get it too hot, you will overcook the eggs and make them a rubbery mess. When the eggs are almost totally set, place the ham, turkey, bacon, and cheese on one side of the eggs. If you are like me and enjoy your bacon a little bit chewy, leave the pieces whole. It looks pretty and you get these different pops of bacon with every bite. Fold the omelet over and turn off the heat. Leave the omelet in the pan to allow the cheese to keep melting for a minute or two. Season to taste with salt and pepper.

NOTES:

Fancy Nancy's Crab Dip

I like to use all kinds of store-bought gluten-free crackers to serve this crab dip with. And my preference is to really coat the top of the dip with the cocktail sauce so the creaminess of the cream cheese comes right on through. For my favorite gluten-free cracker brands, take a gander at the resource section in the back of the book.

Serves 8 to 10

¾ cup store-bought whipped cream cheese

3 tablespoons gluten-free mayonnaise (I like Hellmann's)

1 tablespoon lemon juice

Pinch of cayenne pepper

1 pound cooked crab claw meat

Cocktail Sauce (opposite page), for serving

Are you ready for easy and quick? Well, here you go.

In a nice big bowl, mix together the whipped cream cheese, gluten-free mayonnaise, lemon juice, and cayenne pepper. When it's really smooth, fold in the crab claw meat. Transfer to a clear serving dish and top with Cocktail Sauce. Smooth the sauce over the top of the dip, and refrigerate until ready to serve.

NOTES:

Cocktail Sauce

½ cup gluten-free ketchup
(I like Heinz)

1 teaspoon prepared
horseradish

Mix the ketchup with the prepared horseradish until it looks smooth and there aren't any big lumps of horseradish.

NOTES:

_____

_____

_____

_____

_____

_____

Amy's Armadillo Eggs

You want to impress your in-laws? Make these Armadillo Eggs. (Don't be put off by the name. They're essentially browned balls of sausage that have been stuffed with spiced cheese and jalapeños.) Now, I know they are a little more labor intensive than almost all of the other recipes in this book, but they are so worth it, you'll forget all about the work involved. Serve these with my best ever Microwave Queso (page 123) or Buttermilk Dressing (page 113). I like to make the dipping sauce first so all the flavors can get together and make a difference.

Serves 6 to 8 as an appetizer

2 pounds breakfast sausage or mild or spicy Italian sausage

6 ounces cream cheese, at room temperature

½ cup grated yellow Cheddar cheese

2 cloves garlic, minced

2 teaspoons minced cilantro

½ teaspoon cumin

1 green onion, green parts only, sliced thin

Pinch of cayenne pepper

Salt and pepper to taste

6 medium jalapeños, seeded and cut into squares

Buttermilk Dressing (opposite page), for serving

Remove the sausages from their casings.

In a large mixing bowl, stir together the cream cheese, Cheddar cheese, garlic, cilantro, cumin, green onion, cayenne, and salt and pepper to taste. Mix until as smooth as you can get it. Sometimes you need to get a fork in on the action to smash up the big bits of cream cheese if it's a little hard when you first get going.

Preheat the oven to 375°F.

Now take those little squares of jalapeños and top with a teaspoon-sized dollop of the cream cheese filling. Then take 2 tablespoons of the sausage and form it into a patty. Place the jalapeño in the center of the sausage, fold the sausage up and around the jalapeño, and then form it into a ball. I like to get my hands a little wet before I do this so the sausage won't stick.

Place your newly made armadillo eggs in a roasting pan or on a cookie sheet lined with aluminum foil. Bake for 20 to 30 minutes, until the armadillo eggs are cooked through and nice and browned.

Remove from the oven and serve on a platter with some toothpicks and my Buttermilk Dressing, or your sauce of choice.

NOTES:

_____

_____

Buttermilk Dressing

½ cup gluten-free
mayonnaise
(I like Hellmann's)

1 teaspoon lemon juice

⅓ to ½ cup gluten-free
buttermilk

2 teaspoons cilantro

½ teaspoon salt

¼ teaspoon pepper

In a medium bowl, using a fork or a whisk, stir the gluten-free mayonnaise into the lemon juice and buttermilk. Add the cilantro, salt, and pepper, and mix until smooth. Set aside so all the flavors can get together before you use it.

NOTES:

Spinach Artichoke Dip Done Right

Remember how I told you I was bruising up like a peach when I first got diagnosed? Well, I needed iron, and good thing spinach has so much in it. It was the perfect excuse to whip up a few batches of this just to make sure I hadn't lost my touch. For me, when the going gets tough, the tough get cookin'.

Serves 6

Unsalted butter
for greasing dish

1 (8-ounce) package cream cheese, at room temperature

½ cup gluten-free mayonnaise
(I like Hellmann's)

½ teaspoon salt

½ teaspoon ground black pepper

1 teaspoon onion powder

⅛ teaspoon gluten-free Worcestershire sauce
(I like Lea & Perrins)

¾ cup shredded mozzarella cheese

1½ cups chopped frozen spinach, thawed

1 (14-ounce) can artichoke hearts, drained and chopped

½ cup grated Parmesan cheese

Tortilla chips, for serving

Preheat the oven to 350°F. Lightly grease a 4-quart baking dish with butter.

In a large bowl with a handheld mixer, whip the cream cheese until nice and smooth. Add the gluten-free mayonnaise, salt, pepper, onion powder, Worcestershire sauce, and mozzarella cheese, and mix just until combined. Stir in the thawed spinach and the artichoke hearts until uniform.

Pour into your prepared pan, and smooth with the back of a spoon so it's level. Sprinkle with the Parmesan cheese. Bake for 20 minutes, until the dip is golden and bubbly.

Serve with tortilla chips while the dip is still hot.

Will keep for up to a week in the fridge.

NOTES:

Devils on Horseback

If you're feeling a little devilish for dinner or that dinner party, these always get the gums flapping. Ronnie likes these with the peppered bacon, but they sure do get my motor running with any ol' bacon. You can also make these using prunes, but in that version you have to cut the bacon into smaller strips and use toothpicks to keep it all hanging together. See page 91 for my tips on cooking bacon.

Serves 3

⅓ cup goat cheese
or cream cheese

6 Medjool dates
(the big ones)

6 skinless almonds (also
called blanched almonds)

6 strips of peppered bacon,
fried but not yet crispy

Preheat the oven to 375°F.

In a medium bowl, beat the goat cheese or cream cheese until it's as smooth as you can get it. Cut the dates in half lengthwise, but not all the way through—just enough to get that pit out.

Now spoon a small amount of the goat cheese into each date, and then press an almond into the cheese. Close the date and wrap it with the bacon, being sure that the two ends meet. Place the dates on a cookie sheet with the ends of the bacon on the underside.

Bake for 5 to 10 minutes, until the bacon is crispy and the dates are nice and warm.

Serve right away! No sauce required.

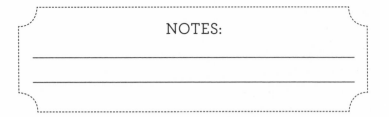

NOTES:

_____

_____

**A lot of people are afraid to say
what they want. That's why they don't
get what they want.**
—Madonna

Frozen Fruit Salad

If you are looking for a recipe that you can make long before your guests arrive, look no further. I can't eat pineapple, so I make mine with canned pears, but my mama makes this with pineapple, so out of respect, I made sure to include her way with mine. If you are in the middle of nowhere and can't find unflavored gelatin, grab a box of Jell-O. I don't recommend blueberry. Serve this salad to friends who love a little retro-style hospitality.

Serves 8 to 10

1 envelope unflavored gelatin

¼ cup cold water

1 (8.5-ounce) can pear halves, diced, or pineapple chunks in heavy syrup, drained and syrup reserved (⅔ cup fruit)

1 cup crushed fresh peaches

1 cup sliced seedless grapes

½ cup maraschino cherries, cut in half

1 cup heavy cream, whipped to soft peaks

3 tablespoons confectioners' sugar

½ cup gluten-free mayonnaise (I like Hellmann's)

In a large glass bowl, soften the gelatin in the cold water, and then heat in the microwave for 30 seconds to dissolve. Add the reserved pear or pineapple syrup. Chill until it begins to thicken up, like 10 minutes.

Whip the heavy cream with the confectioners' sugar until loose folds form.

Add the diced pears or pineapple chunks, peaches, grapes, and cherries, and then fold in the mayonnaise and sweetened whipped cream. Freeze.

For a pretty presentation, divide the salad into clear glasses.

Will keep, covered in the fridge, for up to a week.

NOTES:

Cookie Soup

When you are standing in front of the open refrigerator door and can't think of anything else to snack on, cookie soup is always a good backup plan. Use any kind of milk for the soup part *except* goat milk. Unless, of course, you like your cookies with a side of goat. If you've got a whole houseful of kids like I do, this is the perfect late-night snack for all the kids, big and small.

Serves 3

6 Slice-and-Bake Chocolate Chip Cookies (page 130), or 6 store-bought gluten-free chocolate chip cookies

3 cups almond or regular milk (coconut milk is really good, too)

Crumble up 2 cookies in a tall glass.

Pour 1 cup of milk over it and then stir. Enjoy with a nice big spoon.

In the winter, I like to pop it all in the microwave for warm cookie soup. You can also get creative by experimenting with all kinds of cookies. But I will lay my hand on the Bible every time and say that homemade gluten-free cookies still have the store-bought ones beat by a mile.

NOTES:

_____

_____

_____

_____

_____

_____

Late-Night Twinkies

Close your eyes, 'cause I have a big surprise in store for you! Yes! Gluten-free twinkies are as real as Ronnie Shirley being struck by lightning twice and surviving. Back when I ate gluten, my favorite time to have a Twinkie was late at night, when only Ronnie and the dogs were watching.

Serves 12

¾ cup Amy's Gluten-Free Mix

¾ cup sugar

1 teaspoon baking powder

¼ teaspoon salt

3 tablespoons unsalted butter

3 tablespoons water

4 large eggs, at room temperature, separated

Pinch of cream of tartar

1 tablespoon vanilla extract

4 large eggs, at room temperature, separated

Preheat the oven to 350°F.

First you need to build your twinkie molds, so take that roll of aluminum foil and tear off a piece at least 1 foot long. Fold it in half and then fold it in half again. Now take that spice jar and wrap the foil around it, and then fold in the edges over the ends of the jar so you have something like a tiny feeding trough.

Repeat this step until you have 12 molds.

Now make the batter. In a large bowl, whisk together the gluten-free mix, ¼ cup of the sugar, the baking powder, and the salt and set aside. In a small bowl in the microwave, melt the butter in the water and set aside. In another large bowl in a stand-up mixer with the whisk attachment, whisk the egg whites with the cream of tartar. (Remember, a handheld mixer works just fine as well.) When the egg whites foam up good and are no longer see-through, add ¼ cup of the sugar. Whip the egg whites until they form shiny firm peaks. In another large bowl, add the last ¼ cup of the sugar to the egg yolks, and whip them until pale yellow, about 1 minute.

Whisk the water and melted butter into the egg yolks, and stir to combine. Sprinkle half the dry ingredients over the egg yolk mixture. Using a wooden spoon and some big arm strokes, fold the dry ingredients into the yolks. Now fold the remaining dry ingredients into the whipped egg whites, and then combine the egg yolk mixture with the egg white mixture.

Spoon the batter into the prepared molds and bake for 14 minutes.

FILLING

2 cups heavy cream

2 tablespoons vegetable shortening (I like Crisco)

¾ cup confectioners' sugar

1 teaspoon vanilla extract

Allow the cakes to cool for a few minutes in the molds.

While they cool, make the filling.

Using a handheld mixer, whip the heavy cream with the vegetable shortening, confectioners' sugar, and vanilla extract. Whip until very smooth.

Now, when those cakes are cool, remove one from the mold. Using a skewer, poke three holes in the bottom of one cake. Wiggle it around good to make room for the cream. This is when you have to trust me and your plastic bag. Place the filling in a resealable plastic bag with a plastic tip coming out of one of the corners, and pipe the filling into the cake. Do this right and you will make your mama proud! And your kids will discover a whole new level of gluten-free respect for ya.

These twinkies keep beautifully in an airtight container in the fridge for up to a week.

NOTES:

Puredee Pretzel Bites

Whenever I take my kids to Costco or the mall, they are always asking me for soft pretzels. Only sweet baby Jesus (and maybe every single employee at Costco) knows how much I love those pretzels with the big ol' pieces of salt covering the tops. Those pretzels were one of my favorite treats to get before giving up the gluten. Now I can finally have them, just not when I'm walking through the store, and with smaller pieces of salt. These are bite-size, so they are easier to make.

Serves 6 to 8

3 teaspoons active dry yeast

3 cups Amy's Gluten-Free Mix

2 tablespoons sugar

¾ cup lukewarm water

2 large eggs

2 teaspoons salt

Unsalted butter for greasing bowl

8 cups water

¼ cup honey

¼ cup baking soda

1 large egg white, whisked

Coarse salt for sprinkling

In the large bowl of a stand-up mixer, mix together the yeast, gluten-free mix, and sugar. Add the lukewarm water and eggs. Mix very well until very thick, then add the salt and mix some more until you are pretty much kneading the dough.

Butter a bowl and then transfer the dough into it. Cover with plastic and refrigerate for 1 hour.

Remove from the fridge and preheat the oven to 425°F.

Prepare the water bath: Pour 8 cups of water into a large pot, and add the honey and baking soda. It will fizz up like crazy, which is just what you're looking for.

Now knead the dough into ropes and cut off 1-inch sections.

Allow the dough to rise for 20 minutes, and then drop the pieces into the simmering water bath a few at a time until they puff up big. Remove from the bath and transfer to a cookie sheet. Brush the tops with the egg white, and sprinkle with salt. Bake until golden brown, about 15 to 20 minutes.

Serve with mustard and some Microwave Queso (page 123).

Will keep for a couple of days in a resealable plastic bag.

NOTES:

Onion Dip

My mama would use the Lipton onion soup mix to make her onion dip, but it's not certified gluten-free, so I had to get clever with my taste buds. The kids say it tastes just like the Lipton version, but I think they are just being nice. Ronnie said he'd tell me the truth and proceeded to eat just about the whole bowl with a bag of potato chips. I told him he clearly was lying because he didn't eat it with a bag of Fritos.

Serves 6 to 8

4 ounces cream cheese, at room temperature

½ cup sour cream

½ cup dried onion flakes

3 tablespoons gluten-free beef bouillon powder

¾ teaspoon onion powder

¼ teaspoon celery seed, crushed

¼ teaspoon sugar

1 teaspoon lemon juice

Salt and pepper to taste

Put the cream cheese in a food processor and pulse until the cheese is nice and smooth. Add the sour cream, onion flakes, bouillon powder, onion powder, celery seed, sugar, and lemon juice, and pulse again until silky smooth. If you don't have a food processor, just make sure the cream cheese is nice and soft before you begin stirring. There is nothing worse than having lumps of cream cheese mess up the consistency of the dip. Season to taste with salt and pepper, and your train will be ready to leave the station.

Serve with some good potato chips or Fritos.

Will keep in an airtight container in the fridge for up to a week.

NOTES:

Quick Nachos

When my kids just can't wait for the dinner bell to ring, I whip up a batch of these lightning-fast nachos until dinner is served. I've got a friend that is from New Jersey, and there they call lightning-fast nachos Jersey Nachos because there just ain't that much to them. If you've got spicy heat fiends among your brood, don't be shy about tossing some pickled jalapeño slices over the top of these before nuking them.

Serves 2 to 3

Handful of tortilla chips

½ cup canned refried beans

½ cup shredded Cheddar cheese

½ cup shredded Colby cheese

⅓ cup pico de gallo (store-bought is good enough)

Cover a 12-inch plate with tortilla chips. Spread a small amount of beans over the top of each chip. Sprinkle with the Cheddar and Colby cheese, and pop into the microwave on High for 30 seconds. Check to see if the cheese is fully melted, which it should be. If not, nuke it for 5 to 7 seconds more.

Remove from the microwave and serve with the pico de gallo. Best enjoyed right out of the reactor.

For even faster nachos, leave off the beans and just go with the cheese.

NOTES:

Microwave Queso

If you've got kids, then you've got a queso problem you need solved, since Velveeta isn't gluten-free. If I could hand out a Bum Steer Award, it would be to Velveeta, because how in the good Lord's name is the original blood mud not gluten-free? They need to hire someone to fix that problem, stat! In the meantime, here's my country-fried solution!

Serves 6 to 8

4 cups shredded extra-sharp Cheddar cheese

2 cups shredded Monterey Jack cheese

1½ tablespoons cornstarch

⅓ cup milk

5 ounces (½ can) Ro-Tel Original or Spicy

Tortilla chips, for serving

Place all of the shredded cheese in a bowl, and toss in the cornstarch. Place in the microwave and nuke for 45 seconds on High. Remove from the microwave, add the milk, and stir. Heat for 2 minutes on Medium, take the dip out of the oven, stir in the Ro-Tel, and then heat on Medium for 45 seconds more.

Serve with tortilla chips.

Best enjoyed the day the queso is made.

NOTES:

_____

_____

_____

_____

_____

_____

Lizard-Licking Flour Tortillas

Yes, even country-posh people know that the best quesadillas are made with flour tortillas, so I went ahead and made some gluten-free ones for ya. For fun, you can even add a few drops of green food coloring if you want to have some lizard-looking quesadillas. They match Ronnie's tattoos perfectly.

Makes 12 tortillas

1 tablespoon lard

2¾ cups Amy's Gluten-Free Mix, plus more for dusting

1 teaspoon salt

1¼ teaspoons baking powder

¾ to 1 cup water

In a large bowl, cut the lard into the gluten-free mix, salt, and baking powder with your fingers until you can't see the big lumps of lard anymore. Add the water and stir with a spoon until very thick and sticky. Dust the dough with some more of the gluten-free mix, and knead for a couple of minutes in the bowl until the dough feels smooth and elastic.

Divide the dough into 12 uniform sections (about 45 grams each if you've got a scale handy).

Lightly dust your counter with more of the gluten-free mix. Use a rolling pin to roll out your tortillas (or if you're fancy, use a tortilla press) until they are nice and thin.

Heat a skillet or frying pan over medium heat until piping hot. Cook the tortillas until you get those pretty little brown spots to form. Flip the tortillas and cook the other side the same way. Transfer to a plate. Repeat until all of your dough has been cooked.

Will keep in a resealable plastic bag overnight.

Tortilla Tip: You know I've got no shame when it comes to a good microwave shortcut, and here's one for flour tortillas. First of all, tortillas are best stored in a resealable plastic bag in the refrigerator. Only problem is, they can still become rubbery and/or dry. So if you need to reheat them to make tacos, for example, wrap a stack of 5 or so tortillas in a slightly damp paper towel and pop them in the microwave on High for 40 seconds. They'll be softened, warm, and good to go.

NOTES:

_____

_____

_____

_____

_____

_____

Super Bowl Five-Layer Dip

I don't know about you, but I love me a good layered dip; just make sure you've got some chips that can handle the heavy lifting. There is nothing more annoying than having your chip break off every time you try to pick up some of this simple gift from heaven. The best part of this recipe is that it's kind of like a pattern more than anything. You can add to it or you can take away from it. It all depends on how serious the football game is. I like to add roasted corn, for example, but my favorite add-ons are hearty ground hamburger meat and crispy iceberg lettuce. I like to put the hamburger meat in between the beans and the Cheddar cheese layers and then the iceberg between the cheese and the sour cream layers. I prefer to make this on a platter for optimal chip access to the layers, but if you're traveling with it, a glass casserole dish can do the trick and show off those pretty layers, too.

Serves 6

1 (14-ounce) can
refried beans

1 (4-ounce) can chopped
green chiles

6 shakes of ground cumin

½ teaspoon onion powder

1½ cups finely shredded
sharp Cheddar cheese

1 cup sour cream

1 cup pico de gallo
(store-bought is fine)

1 cup guacamole
(store-bought is fine)

1 cup Monterey Jack cheese

1 (4-ounce) can sliced
black olives

Dump the refried beans in a bowl and stir in the green chiles, cumin, and onion powder. Mix this up real good, and then pour it onto the bottom of a serving platter. I really don't like putting this in a bowl, because it's just too hard to get to every layer when your chip can't reach it. Everyone just starts asking for a napkin.

So spread those beans out until they are smooth. Then sprinkle on the Cheddar cheese. Spread the sour cream over the cheese.

Take ½ cup of the pico de gallo and mix it into the guacamole, and then spread this over the sour cream. Add another layer of the pico de gallo, then sprinkle the Monterey Jack cheese over that. Top with the sliced black olives and serve.

Nothing looks more like yum than this dip in the middle of your coffee table.

Leftovers will keep for a couple of days in the fridge.

NOTES:

_____

_____

String-Cheese Quesadillas

I like to make tortillas the day before so I can whip up some quesadillas for the kids as a snack when they get home from school. They come in equally handy when I use them for suppertime.

Serves 6

3 tablespoons unsalted butter

12 of my homemade tortillas (page 124) or store-bought gluten-free corn tortillas

6 mozzarella string cheeses, peeled into strips or cut into pieces

2 cups shredded Monterey Jack cheese

2 cups shredded white Cheddar cheese

1 cup pico de gallo (optional)

1 cup shredded cooked chicken (optional)

Heat your skillet over medium heat, and then add ½ tablespoon of the unsalted butter. When the butter has melted, take one of the gluten-free flour tortillas and place it into your hot skillet. Pile it with one-sixth of the mozzarella, and then top that with a generous handful of shredded cheese. Add pico de gallo or shredded cooked chicken, if you like. Place another tortilla on top of the filling, and then flip it and cook that side until the cheese is completely melted and the tortillas are slightly crunchy.

Repeat this process until all of your tortillas are used up or until you run out of cheese, whichever comes first.

Cut into wedges and serve.

NOTES:

Tuna Melt

Okay, now there aren't a ton of sandwiches in this book, but I am most definitely a sandwich eater, and this is one of my all-time favorites. Sometimes the only meat we had in our pantry when it was just me and my mama were cans of Spam and tuna fish. Let's just say that my mama taught me the best ways to prepare both. For a fun Spam recipe, see page 141.

To this day, I have yet to meet a tuna melt that lasts more than 20 minutes. Sad as it is true, tuna melts really don't keep well. The bread gets soggy and having to reheat it is never pretty, so come hungry and go home on a full tank.

Serves 6

6 slices Donna D's Honey'd Oat Bread (page 58), or store-bought gluten-free bread

2 to 3 tablespoons of gluten-free mayonnaise for spreading (I like Hellmann's)

1 recipe Tuna Salad (page 97)

12 slices Cheddar cheese

Salt and pepper to taste

First, toast the bread. Then smear gluten-free mayonnaise on one side of each piece. Pile some tuna salad on a slice of the bread with the mayo side up, dust the tuna with a little salt and pepper, and then place two pieces of cheese on top of the salad. Microwave the sandwich for 45 seconds, until the cheese has melted. Call me old-fashioned, but I like to serve my tuna melts open-faced so it's less about the bread and more about the salad. If you disagree, just toast up twelve pieces of bread instead of six.

If you're a caveman and don't have a microwave yet, just put your tuna melt on a cookie sheet in a 500°F oven until the cheese melts—which won't take long.

NOTES:

_____
_____
_____
_____
_____
_____

Broccoli Cheese Dip

Now I usually eat broccoli only in my salads, but when it comes down to it, if I'm just hanging in there like a hair in a biscuit after a long day and need to bring something with a vegetable in it to Ronnie's parents' house (that I know my kids will eat), I always whip up this broccoli cheese dip. Sure, the broccoli is floating in a sea of cheese, but you know what? That casserole dish is never still full by the time we sit down to sup.

Serves 8 as a starter

1 tablespoon unsalted butter, plus extra for greasing dish

3 stalks celery, chopped

1 onion, chopped small

1 (10-ounce) package frozen chopped broccoli, cooked and drained

1 (10.75-ounce) can gluten-free cream of mushroom soup

1 (8-ounce) package cream cheese, at room temperature

1 teaspoon garlic powder

5 ounces (½ can) Ro-Tel tomatoes (optional)

Salt and pepper to taste

Tabasco sauce to taste

Gluten-free toast triangles, tortilla chips, or rice crackers, for serving

Grease an 8-inch square casserole dish with butter and set aside.

Melt 1 tablespoon unsalted butter in a cast-iron skillet over medium heat, and then add the celery and onion. Cook until the celery is soft and the onion is translucent. Stir in the broccoli, cream of mushroom soup, cream cheese, garlic powder, and Ro-Tel tomatoes, if using. Mix just until smooth, and then remove the skillet from the heat. Adjust the seasoning with the salt, pepper, and Tabasco sauce, and then pour into your prepared casserole dish.

Serve with gluten-free toast triangles or tortilla chips or rice crackers.

Will keep good for a couple of days.

NOTES:

Slice-and-Bake Chocolate Chip Cookies

It's late at night and nothing else sounds good except some freshly baked cookies. And not just any cookie. I'm talking about a cookie of the slice-and-bake variety, and let me tell you, folks, these gluten-free slice-and-bake cookies will make you think it's Christmas every day of the year. In fact, we should all keep a log of these in the freezer, ready to go when we need a little Santa in our lives. Ho! Ho! Ho! It's cookie time! Where's my milk?

Makes 4 dozen cookies

8 tablespoons unsalted butter, diced

¾ cup granulated sugar

¾ cup firmly packed light brown sugar

1 large egg

1 large egg yolk

1 tablespoon vanilla extract

2½ cups Amy's Gluten-Free Mix

1 teaspoon baking powder

¼ teaspoon salt

1 tablespoon almond or regular milk (plus more for serving)

1 (12-ounce) bag semisweet chocolate chips

½ cup chopped pecans (optional)

In a large bowl using your handheld mixer, cream together the butter and the sugars. Add the egg and the yolk, and mix until smooth. Stir in the vanilla extract. In another bowl, combine the gluten-free mix with the baking powder and salt. Sift this mix over the butter and sugar mix. Stir until nice and thick. Add the milk. Stir in the chocolate chips and the pecans, if desired. Then cover the dough and refrigerate it for 2 hours. Remove from the fridge and lightly dust the counter with additional gluten-free mix or tapioca starch. Roll the dough into 2 separate logs. Cover with plastic wrap. Freeze until ready to use.

Preheat the oven to 350°F. Line your cookie sheets with parchment paper.

Slice off ½-inch sections of dough, and stagger them on the cookie sheet with at least 1 inch between the cookies. Bake for 10 to 15 minutes, until the cookies are set and golden.

Serve with cool milk.

These babies keep great in a resealable plastic bag on the counter for a week—if the kids don't eat them first.

NOTES:

_____

_____

SUPPERTIME

Suppertime is my favorite time of day. Not just because that means the day is done, but because it makes me think of my grandma telling me, "Get in here, it's time to sup!" Then the whole family would settle in around the table and we would talk about our day. Thankfully, Ronnie and I are of the same mind when it comes to this tradition, because even when life is crazier than a bull in a china closet, our suppers taste just a little bit better with us all together. Come to think of it, I realized I had fallen in love with Ronnie over one of the recipes I included in here, so keep reading to unravel that yarn.

> # The secret of getting ahead is getting started.
> • • • • •
> **—Mark Twain**

When I look at all the recipes that make up this chapter, I can't help but smile because it makes me realize I went all out and included a little bit of everything I love to make gluten-free. I did some fancy date-night dishes like my Jalapeño Shrimp and Cilantro Rice (page 154) and threw in some of my all-time favorite comfort foods like my Crispy Corncob Corn Bread (page 156) and Old-Timey Celery Soup (page 139) to show that I mean what I say: gluten-free can be flat-out finger-licking good if you really want it to be.

I hear from so many of my fans that they are sad that they are gluten-free because their suppertime isn't what it used to be: just brambles and fishing hooks. Well, dry your eyes and pull those sad hooks from your mouths, because suppertime is about to get as shiny as a brand-new chrome bumper.

My
Homegrown History

In the summertime, when I was real little, you'd find me snappin' beans or shuckin' corn because almost everything we had to eat on the table came out of the garden (or it had been frozen in the deep freezer but originally came out of the garden). I lived on a 65-acre farm, and we had our own cows and pigs. I think, honestly, if we went back to that old way of cooking, when we had to grow our own vegetables and keep chickens for eggs and have a potato house that we'd drag the potatoes out of, people would not be having so many food allergies because there wouldn't be so many preservatives added to the food in the first place to be allergic to! It's a running joke in my family that my mama is seventy-three years old but she acts like she's fifty-five. In her time, everything she made or prepared was done strictly from scratch; you knew what was in it, and it was homegrown.

My grandfather and my grandmama had eight kids, so my mama had a very large family. All the kids were the farmhands working their land. When I was about four my family started to sell off the animals, because by that point you could go straight to the supermarket to get everything instead of putting in all the labor. But the old homestead is still standing at the end of perhaps the only dirt road left in Wake Forest, North Carolina, and the family has moved back in. Every Saturday all the brothers and sisters that are still living get together and eat Saturday lunch together.

I know it's this part of me that got me hankering for a part of that back in our daily rotation, so a couple of years ago, Ronnie and I decided to do a garden in our backyard. It's better when you have more people helping, I believe, and some people are not, um . . . as green thumb as they think they are. But we had some good corn and it was the first time I'd ever grown carrots. It was cool and the kids really liked it. We try to intertwine some of our upbringing into our kids' lives so that if we're ever not around they at least have a little history and knowledge to pass on to their kids. We do it as a project nowadays, but back then, it was just how we lived.

My mother raised three girls on her own from the time I was four. And by the time I was eight, my sister Nancy (who is ten years older) and my sister Donna (who is fifteen years my senior) were out of the house, so she took a lot of time teaching me things when it came to cookin'. Anything I needed to know about life, she was there. Today she's kind of like the old woman who lives in the shoe. All her grandkids and my cousins' kids all come to her house.

I like to cook, but I love to bake more than anything, and when I was pregnant with my second child, Maggie, I prayed and prayed for a girl (but I figured she was going to be a boy because my two sisters each have two boys). God answered my prayers and gave me a girl, and she's the biggest girlie girl. She likes to do nothing but things like bake and garden, so now it's just a matter of finding the time to pass what my mother taught me on to her. Alexa and my baby girl, Maggie, are really crafty and love doing family projects. They kinda like that old way of life. (In fact, Maggie was talking about having a greenhouse just the other day, but then she realized that she had to get plants!) It's really important to me that even though I can't come out and plow a twenty-row garden, I can come out and do about four rows and try to teach my kids some of what I learned when I was a kid.

Between my mom, my grandmother, and my great-aunts, I never needed for anything growing up. (What I *wanted* was a different story.) But I guess the best things you can give your kids in life are clean clothes and love. There's so much meanness and hatred in the world, so you better let them know that no matter what, you're gonna be there for them. People get caught up in their lives and forget that. When Ronnie came around, we always said it's us against the world, and we still do. We get criticized a whole lot and called out a whole lot on things that we do, but I tell Ronnie, just let them say what they want to if it makes them feel better. People talk about having riches and gold, but if you don't have a family or someone like my mother who is there for you, then you don't know what riches and gold are. People like that are irreplaceable. You can get a new ring or a new car, but you can't get a new mom or a new grandmother. I may never have been able to have a Louis Vuitton bag until now, but you know, I don't even really want it. As long as my bag holds everything I need, I'm good. The best things in life are free—your traditions, your love, and what's passed down. You can't buy those things, and to me "homegrown" memories and love are the real treasure. And all of these things come out in the food we eat, which makes this collection of recipes a real piece of my heart.

SUPPERTIME

Hominy Casserole

The great thing about being in the South is, even if you don't know a whole heck of a lot about food, if you say it's got corn in it, people will eat it. Hominy is like corn, only bigger and softer. Of course I'm gonna tell you to use bread crumbs from *my* bread, but store-bought gluten-free bread crumbs work just as good for this casserole.

Serves 6

3 to 4 tablespoons unsalted butter

3 (15-ounce) cans hominy, drained and rinsed

3 (4.5-ounce) cans chopped green chiles

Salt and pepper to taste

1½ cups grated Cheddar cheese

½ cup gluten-free bread crumbs (use Donna D's Honey'd Oat Bread, page 58)

¾ cup heavy cream or full-fat coconut milk

Preheat the oven to 350°F. Butter a 14 × 10 × 2-inch roasting pan.

Spoon a layer of the hominy over the bottom of the pan, then dot with pinches of unsalted butter and scoops of the green chiles. Sprinkle with salt and pepper, and then top with some of the cheese. Keep doing this until all of your ingredients are used up, making sure your last layer is the hominy.

Sprinkle the bread crumbs over the top of the hominy, and then pour the cream or coconut milk all over.

Bake for 20 minutes, or until the cheese is melted and the bread crumbs are golden.

Will keep for a week in the fridge.

NOTES:

Old-Timey Celery Soup

I love all kinds of soup for all kinds of reasons. Soups are comforting and can feed a whole army if you double the recipe enough times. But they are also bright and do something magical to your insides. Celery soup is older than dirt and refreshing as a rainstorm. My mama said that it's been around since the dawn of time because it's just that good. Now how can anyone argue with that?

Serves 6

2 cups chicken stock

2 cups water

3 cups finely sliced celery, leaves included

2 tablespoons unsalted butter

1 cup minced onion

3 tablespoons cornstarch

2 cups milk

1 cup cream

1 teaspoon Season-All Seasoned Salt

Ground black pepper to taste

In a large stockpot, bring the chicken stock and the water to a boil over high heat. Add the celery and boil for 3 minutes, then reduce to a simmer and cover with a lid. Simmer for 15 minutes.

In the meantime, melt the butter in a large skillet over medium heat, and then cook the onion down until translucent. Add the cornstarch and milk, and whisk until thick. Remove from the heat.

Using a hand blender, blend the celery and stock until smooth. (You can use a regular blender if you work in small batches, but be very careful of that hot liquid.) Pour the celery into the onion mixture and stir to combine. Add the heavy cream and the Season-All Seasoned Salt. Add pepper (and salt if needed) to taste.

Serve warm.

Throw any extra into a Thermos and you've got lunch for tomorrow.

NOTES:

_____

_____

_____

_____

Alexa's Best Ever Meatloaf

I named this after my daughter Alexa because it is hands down her favorite dinner. It tastes good hot or cold, and it makes a mean sandwich when you are thinking of the other main food group. My mama used to make her meatloaf with saltines, but since those aren't gluten-free and I don't have time to make them from scratch, this is the best solution I've found yet. Glutino makes the right crackers for this recipe. You can be sure as a thunderstorm that rice crackers will not work here.

Serves 6 to 8

1 pound ground pork

1 pound ground beef

3 cloves garlic, minced

1 (4.4-ounce) box gluten-free table crackers, crushed (about ½ cup; I like Glutino)

2 large eggs

¼ cup chopped black olives

3 tablespoons tomato paste

1½ teaspoons salt

½ teaspoon pepper

1 teaspoon dried thyme

3 tablespoons fresh parsley

6 or 7 slices thick-cut bacon, like applewood smoked

½ cup gluten-free ketchup (optional)

Preheat the oven to 350°F. Line a 14 × 10 × 2-inch roasting pan with foil.

Mix the pork, beef, garlic, crushed crackers, eggs, olives, tomato paste, salt, pepper, thyme, and parsley with your hands until the mixture looks the same throughout.

Shape the meat into a loaf that looks like a fat football; you want your rectangle to have tapered ends. Place the loaf in the roasting pan.

Lay the bacon, with each piece overlapping the one before it, over the top of the meatloaf, and tuck the ends up under the loaf. Spread ketchup over the top of the meatloaf if you wish.

Bake for 1 hour and 30 minutes. Allow the pan to sit on the counter to cool for 10 minutes. Slice and serve with some ketchup.

NOTES:

_____

_____

Life expands and contracts in direct proportion to one's courage.

—Anaïs Nin

Twice-Baked Spam-tatoes

I laugh out loud every time I make this recipe for suppertime, because after going gluten-free I was sure I wouldn't ever be able to have Spam again. When I found out it was gluten-free, I called my mama to tell her the good news.

Serves 4

4 large Idaho potatoes

4 tablespoons unsalted butter

1 cup shredded Cheddar cheese or cheese substitute, plus more for topping

4 strips crisp-cooked bacon, chopped

1 green onion, chopped

1 (12-ounce) can Spam, diced

½ cup sour cream (optional)

Poke holes in the potatoes after you have scrubbed and dried them. Microwave them for 7 to 8 minutes on High. Remove from the microwave and let them cool until you can touch them without burning your puppy paws.

Cut the potatoes in half lengthwise and scoop out the insides. Mash the insides with the butter, cheese, crispy bacon, green onion, and diced Spam. Mix together real good, and when it's smooth enough, spoon it back into the potato skins.

Sprinkle with a little extra cheese if you like, and pop them back into the microwave and nuke them for 1 minute more, until the cheese has melted. Serve with or without the sour cream.

Leftovers keep just fine for a few days in a sealed container in the fridge.

NOTES:

_____

_____

_____

_____

_____

_____

Beef Tips with Rice

My favorite kinds of dishes to make are the ones that smell so good that when you walk into the house, the aromas just wrap you up in a blanket and curl your eyelashes. My Beef Tips with Rice is one of those recipes—and for good reason. It's very popular in the Carolinas, and I'm pretty sure that's because everyone in the Carolinas loves a moment that curls their eyelashes.

I've used round steak here, but truth be told, just about any cut of beef that you can find on sale is fine and will become just as tender and good. Like when we roast our pigs, remember—low and slow wins the race. That is key to serving up the best southern comfort food.

Serves 6

FOR THE MEAT

**1 pound round steak,
cut into 1-inch cubes**

Salt and pepper

1 tablespoon vegetable oil

1 tablespoon unsalted butter

2 small onions, sliced

6 cloves garlic, minced

3 cups beef broth

Put your cubed meat in a bowl and generously dust it with salt and pepper. Toss the cubes to make sure the meat is evenly coated.

In a nice big pot over medium heat, heat 1 tablespoon of vegetable oil with 1 tablespoon of unsalted butter. When the butter is melted, add the cubed meat and sauté until brown, stirring that pot often so the meat doesn't stick.

Add the sliced onions and the minced garlic, and cook just until the onions become translucent, something like 5 to 7 minutes. Add ½ teaspoon each salt and pepper and stir good.

Add the beef broth, stir a couple of times, bring to a boil, and then cover with a tight-fitting lid. Reduce the heat to a simmer and cook for at least 2 hours. Come back, give it a good stir, and add more salt and pepper to taste. Give the meat a taste, and if it's as tender as you want it, then move on. Sometimes I like to cook it another hour, but that just depends on the meat and my mood.

Now make the rice. Rinse the rice so it won't turn into a giant rice blob when you cook it.

FOR THE RICE

1 cup rice

2¼ cups water

1 tablespoon unsalted butter

1 teaspoon salt

**Splash of rice vinegar
(any vinegar will do)**

¼ cup cornstarch

Salt and pepper to taste

Pour 1¾ cups water into a saucepan with a lid. Add the rice, butter, salt, and a splash of vinegar (a splash in the ladylike way, meaning less than a teaspoon, not a shot glass full).

Bring the rice to a boil over high heat, and then cover with foil and the lid. Reduce the temperature to a simmer and leave it alone for 15 minutes.

While you are waiting, put the cornstarch in a small bowl and cover with ½ cup cold water. Stir until very smooth. Pour this mixture into the beef tips and stir until the gravy thickens up. Season to taste with salt and pepper as needed.

When the rice is done, fluff it with a fork, then spoon some into a bowl and top with the beef tips. Yum.

Any extra will keep in a plastic container tucked into the fridge for a week.

NOTES:

Tuna Tetrazzini Casserole

When it comes to a classic hot dish, Tuna Tetrazzini is one of the first that come to mind. I've seen it served with potato chips and everything in between, but I prefer mine shooting straight from the hip. If you've got it in your mind to plan ahead, do all the steps up until baking, then cover and refrigerate, and you can bake it the next day. I'm pretty sure that's what they call looking like you can do it all.

Serves 8

3 tablespoons unsalted butter

1 large onion

½ cup minced red bell pepper

3 cloves garlic, minced

1 cup sliced white mushrooms

¾ teaspoon dried thyme

¼ teaspoon dried oregano

½ teaspoon paprika

⅛ teaspoon cayenne pepper

½ teaspoon onion powder

½ cup white wine

2 cups chicken stock

1½ cups half-and-half

3 tablespoons cornstarch

Salt and pepper to taste

2 cans tuna fish

1 pound gluten-free pasta, cooked

¾ cup grated Parmesan cheese

In a large stockpot over medium heat, melt the butter. When it foams, add the onion and bell pepper. Cook until the onion turns clear, and then add the garlic, mushrooms, thyme, oregano, paprika, cayenne, and onion powder.

Cook for 3 minutes, being sure to stir it often. Add the white wine, chicken stock, and half-and-half. Cook for 2 minutes, and then pour a little of the liquid mixture into a small glass bowl with the cornstarch. Stir to dissolve the cornstarch, and pour this mixture back into the pot. Stir to combine and season to taste with salt and pepper.

Preheat the oven to 350°F.

Cook over medium heat until the mixture is nice and thick, stirring often.

Remove from the heat, and stir in the tuna and the noodles. Pour the Tetrazzini in a 14 × 10 × 2-inch roasting pan and sprinkle with the Parmesan cheese.

Bake for 20 minutes, or until the cheese is bubbly.

Serve right away!

Leftovers? What leftovers?

NOTES:

_____

_____

Cheddar Chicken and Rice Casserole

One of the things I missed the most when I first went gluten-free was canned cream of mushroom soup and canned corn chowder. Luckily, they have a gluten-free version of both, so now I can stop sending all those nasty letters to Campbell's. Progresso beat them to the punch. This is a great way to use a little leftover rice, and you can prep this ahead and pop it in the oven for a really quick meal.

Serves 8

Unsalted butter for greasing dish

1 cup rice, cooked

½ green bell pepper, diced

1 small (4-ounce) jar pimientos

1 can (18.5-ounce) gluten-free chicken and corn chowder (I like Progresso)

½ cup shredded Colby cheese

Salt and pepper to taste

1½ cups shredded Cheddar cheese

Preheat the oven to 350°F. Grease a 13 x 9 x 2-inch casserole dish with unsalted butter.

Stir the cooked rice with the bell pepper, pimientos, and chowder. Add the Colby cheese next, and then season to taste with the salt and pepper. I like to start off with ¼ teaspoon of each and then go from there.

Pour the mixture into the prepared casserole dish, and then sprinkle with the Cheddar cheese.

Bake the casserole for 20 to 25 minutes, until the cheese is lightly browned and bubbly.

Serve immediately, but be sure to warn everyone that it is molten lava hot! You want to make their taste buds sing, not burn them off.

It doesn't take a rocket scientist to figure out how to store this one. Just don't eat it when you find it in your fridge a month later.

NOTES:

_____

_____

_____

_____

Mashed Potatoes

When I have a smidge more time on my hands and I don't make my Hungry Jack Potatoes, I like to make my mashed potatoes from scratch. This is my and my family's favorite way to do it. When I'm feeling fancy, I like to add crumbled-up bacon and sometimes blue cheese. But you can add anything from shredded Parmesan to chopped green onions or roasted garlic, as you please.

Serves 4

6 large russet potatoes

½ cup (1 stick) salted butter

¼ to 1 cup half-and-half

Additional salt, if needed

Peel and cube the potatoes. Boil in salted water until fork tender, and then drain. Mash the potatoes with a masher. In a large bowl using a handheld mixer, whip the potatoes with the butter, starting out with ¼ cup half-and-half. Mix until thick, and then add more half-and-half until it's the consistency you like. I generally like a slightly thicker mashed potato, so I use no more than 1 cup of half-and-half. Season with additional salt if you need to.

When I have leftover mashed potatoes, I like to bake them the next day at 350°F so the top gets a nice crust on it.

NOTES:

_____

_____

_____

_____

_____

_____

Chicken and Pea Pasta Casserole

Casseroles are a working mother's dream dish because you can get the veggies, the meat, and the starches all in the same place at the same time. Kinda like Ronnie when he's repoing a car. Use this easy recipe the way my grandmama used patterns to make clothes—as a template. Toss in leftovers like frozen sliced green beans or asparagus in place of the peas, or roast turkey in place of the chicken.

Serves 6

1 pound gluten-free penne pasta

1 tablespoon unsalted butter, plus additional for pan

1 tablespoon oil

Salt and pepper to taste

½ pound chicken tenderloins

1 (18-ounce) can gluten-free cream of mushroom soup

2 cups frozen peas

2 cups shredded American cheese

First, in a large stockpot filled with water with 1 tablespoon of salt, cook the pasta until it's al dente—just the right consistency, not too soft. Drain the pasta and rinse.

Preheat the oven to 350°F. Butter a 13 × 9 × 2-inch casserole pan.

Melt 1 tablespoon butter with the oil in a large skillet over medium-high heat. Salt and pepper the chicken tenderloins, and then fry them until they are cooked through. Transfer the chicken pieces to your cutting board and cut them into cubes.

In a large bowl, mix the cooked pasta with the cream of mushroom soup. Add the frozen peas and the cubed chicken. Scoop the mixture into the prepared casserole dish, and level the pasta in the pan. Sprinkle the top with the cheese. Bake for 30 minutes, or until the cheese is melted and the casserole is bubbling hot.

Serve right away to smiles around the table.

NOTES:

Finger-Snappin' Split Pea Soup

My grandmama would turn over in her grave if I didn't share her recipe for split pea soup, so to avoid running into her at night, I went ahead and included it. I grew up eating this soup at least once a week because it was so cheap to make. You can literally make it from the scraps in the kitchen, and it freezes up perfectly for future suppers.

Serves 8

1 pound ham hock

2 cups green split peas, rinsed and the bad ones tossed out

2 quarts (8 cups) water

1 large carrot, diced

1 celery rib, diced

2 cloves garlic

1 onion, diced

¼ teaspoon ground cloves

1 bay leaf

Salt to taste

Combine all the ingredients in a large stockpot and bring to a rolling boil. Cover with foil, then place your lid on the pot, making sure the lid seals with the foil. Reduce the heat to simmer, and cook for 2 hours, stirring every once in a while.

Pull out the ham hock and cut off the meat and dice it up. Remove the bay leaf. Puree the soup using a handheld blender or a food processor (in batches if needed), but be careful, it's hot! If you used a food processor, pour the soup back into the pot. Stir in the meat and serve.

I like to freeze single-serving amounts of this soup for days when I just don't know what's gonna happen.

NOTES:

Gluten-Free Hamburger Helper

I grew up eating Hamburger Helper, and since I couldn't eat it anymore, I wanted to make sure my kids could still enjoy it with me. This recipe tastes like it's right out of the box, and my kids? They thought it *was* right out of a box. That, my friends, is what I call gluten-free success.

Makes 8 hearty servings

1 pound ground beef

1½ teaspoons salt

1 tablespoon unsalted butter

2 cups gluten-free elbow macaroni

2½ cups milk

1½ cups hot water

1 tablespoon cornstarch

1 tablespoon chili powder

3 teaspoons garlic powder

2¼ teaspoons onion powder

1 teaspoon sugar

1¾ teaspoons paprika

¼ teaspoon cayenne pepper (optional)

2 cups shredded Cheddar cheese

Sauté the beef in a cast-iron skillet over medium heat until brown. Add the salt and the butter. When the butter has melted, add the pasta, milk, water, cornstarch, and all those yummy spices. Stir them in good so everything tastes the same.

Bring to a low boil, then reduce to a simmer and cover for 25 to 35 minutes. I like to check on the dish and stir it a few times just to make sure the pasta isn't sticking.

Taste the pasta to see if it's tender, and when it is, stir in the Cheddar cheese. Serve immediately.

NOTES:

If you obey all the rules, you miss all the fun.

— Katharine Hepburn

Veg-It-All Beef Soup

One of my all-time favorite easy-as-pie working mama recipes to whip up for dinner is my Veg-It-All Beef Soup. Everything is out of a can or a box (unless you make your own beef stock), and I can pull off a great-tasting dinner in 20 minutes or less. Now you can too!

Serves 6

1 tablespoon oil

1 pound ground beef

Salt and pepper to taste

2 (15-ounce) cans Veg-All Mixed Vegetables

1 cup beef broth

Heat the oil in a large stockpot over medium heat, and then add the ground beef. Season with salt and pepper, and cook the ground beef until it gets a little crispy and brown. Then add the Veg-All Mixed Vegetables and the beef broth. Adjust the seasoning to taste, and serve.

NOTES:

_____

_____

_____

_____

_____

_____

Amy's Chex Crunchy Chicken Tenders

Have you ever had such a stressful day that you wish there really was an erase button? I used to have a bunch of these stress balls that you can squeeze so your head doesn't explode, but now I just make my Chex Crunchy Chicken Tenders when I feel the need to release. Crushing the cereal between my hands is far more satisfying than allowing any type of explosion to occur. Alternatively you can dump the Chex into a large resealable bag and have at it with your fists to crush it down. Take your pick of stress relief! In any case, mine is a southern table, and what kind of southern spread would I have without a bit of fried chicken once in a while? Chex to the rescue, in more than one way.

Serves 6

2 cups gluten-free Rice Chex cereal

1 cup Amy's Gluten-Free Mix

1 teaspoon salt

1 teaspoon black pepper

2 large eggs

1 pound chicken tenderloins

3 cups vegetable oil

Using your hands, crush the Chex into a large bowl, and add the gluten-free mix and the salt and pepper. Pour this mixture into a large roasting pan.

In a large bowl, whisk the eggs, and then dump the chicken pieces into the eggs.

Heat the oil in a large heavy skillet to 350°F. (See my tips for frying on page 49.) Place a brown paper bag on the counter next to where you are working so you can easily put the chicken on it to drain when you are done frying.

One piece at a time, dredge the chicken in the flour coating. I like to really press the coating onto the chicken so it gets a super crunchy bite. Start by frying one piece at a time. Remove from the oil after 3 to 4 minutes, when the tenders are golden brown. Place on the brown paper bag. Repeat, frying no more than 4 tenders at a time.

Serve with Mashed Potatoes (page 146) and green beans.

NOTES:

_____

_____

The Shirley Steamer

I'd never even heard of a steamer until the night Ronnie took me to his parent's house for the first time for dinner. His mother laid the table out just like this: a waxed red-and-white-checkered tablecloth with a giant pot in the middle, filled with steamed crab legs, red potatoes, bite-size corn, shrimp, lobster tails, and scallops. There were a couple of sets of tongs for digging around in the pot with, a wooden bucket for all the shells and throwaway, and then three bowls with melted salted butter. And that was it. I didn't see what was inside the pot until his mama removed the lid when we were all sitting around the table, but it was one of the best meals of my life. It was that night that I knew I was in love with Ronnie Shirley, and it was that night that I realized I had just signed up for crazy. And I mean that in the best possible way.

Serves 6

2 pounds crab legs

2 pounds lobster tails
(or 2 tails)

1 pound red new potatoes,
washed and quartered

1 (15-ounce) can baby corn,
drained

1 pound shrimp

½ pound bay scallops

1 lemon, quartered

2 cups water

1 tablespoon salt

2 tablespoons Old Bay
Seasoning

2 cups (4 sticks) salted
butter, melted

Place crab legs, lobster tails, potatoes, corn, shrimp, scallops, and the lemon in a big steamer bucket. Fill a giant stockpot with 2 cups of water. The water should not touch the bottom of the steamer bucket when you place the bucket in the pot. Dust the ingredients with the salt and the Old Bay Seasoning. Place the bucket in the pot, and place a lid on the pot. Simmer over medium heat until the potatoes are fork tender, about 20 minutes. Steaming makes the seafood very tender, so don't balk at the cooking time.

Serve the steamer right on the table with plenty of melted salted butter.

NOTES:

Bourbon Sweet Potato Surprise

Now don't freak out that I'm about to use a little bourbon to cook with in this recipe. It's one thing to *drink* bourbon and it's a whole other beast when you cook with it. The alcohol burns off while the casserole is cooking, and all that remains is that nectar-sweet taste and a rich fragrance to complement those taters. So embrace that inner redneck and take a walk with me.

Serves 8

6 large sweet potatoes

1¼ teaspoons salt

6 tablespoons salted butter, plus additional for dish

½ teaspoon ground cinnamon

½ teaspoon ground nutmeg

¼ cup heavy cream

1 large egg

½ cup gluten-free bourbon, like Maker's Mark

Sliced almonds or marshmallows (or both!) for topping

Scrub the sweet potatoes and just cut the ends off and leave the skins on. The skins keep the sweet potato flavor in while they boil. Add them to a large pot filled with enough water to cover the potatoes. Add the salt. Over high heat, bring the water to a boil and cook till a fork gives them a run for their money.

Drain the potatoes, and when they are cool enough to touch, remove the skins. They should peel right off.

Preheat the oven to 350°F. Butter an 11 × 7 × 2-inch casserole dish.

Mash the potatoes with a masher or process them in a food processor if you've got one. Mix with the butter, cinnamon, and nutmeg. Add the heavy cream, egg, and bourbon, and mix until very smooth.

Spoon the potato mixture into the dish and smooth the top. Bake for 30 minutes. Remove from the oven and sprinkle with the almonds and the marshmallows if you are using them. Bake for an additional 5 to 8 minutes, or until the marshmallows are lightly browned but not burned.

NOTES:

Jalapeño Shrimp and Cilantro Rice

When it's date night for Ronnie and me, I like to use my special soap to get ready and then whip up this special dinner just for the two of us. But that never happens anymore, so I just make this after Ronnie takes one of his long "calls." That's just code for "gone fishing!" When I prep the jalapeño for this dish, I discard the stem and seeds, but I don't trim out the inner ribs. You want a bit of that heat to get the juices flowing, after all.

Serves 6

FOR THE RICE

1 cup white rice

1¾ cups water

1 teaspoon salt

2 tablespoons unsalted butter

3 tablespoons chopped cilantro

Zest of 1 lime

FOR THE SHRIMP

3 tablespoons unsalted butter

1 onion, minced or grated

2 cloves garlic, crushed and minced

¼ teaspoon red pepper flakes

1 jalapeño or serrano pepper, cut thin

1 (13-ounce) can crushed tomatoes

So to get started, I like to get the rice going first. Rinse the rice until the water runs clear, okay? Then pour it into a saucepan, add the water, salt, and butter. Bring to a boil, then reduce the temperature to low, cover that pot, and let it steam for 15 to 18 minutes.

While that is getting good and hot, I like to whip up the shrimp, because that's how fast this dish is.

I like to cheat and buy the frozen shrimp and defrost them right before I make this. Just fill half your sink with cold water and place a dinner plate over the bags of shrimp.

No matter what, whatever shrimp you use, just make sure they are clean (see my cleaning tips on the next page). In a large stockpot or saucepan over medium heat, melt the butter and add the onion and let that cook for about 3 minutes. Then add the garlic, red pepper flakes, and jalapeño pepper. Cook that for a couple minutes more, then pour in the can of tomatoes and the chicken broth. Raise the heat to a boil and boil the liquid for 10 minutes to reduce it down and make the flavor more intense. Add the shrimp and cook just until the shrimp are done; bright pink is more like it! Add the lime juice.

Now don't forget to add the cilantro and lime zest to that rice. Give it a good stir, and then spoon a big old hunk of that rice onto a plate and top with those shrimp. So simple, yet so good, y'all!

1 cup chicken broth

2 pounds peeled and deveined shrimp

Juice of 1 lime

Shrimp Tip: It's a whole lot less expensive to peel and devein the shrimp yourself, so it's worth it to learn how. Start by pulling the head off, and then pull the main back shell off. Next pinch off the legs and the tail if you're not keeping that part on. Then take a paring knife and make a shallow slit down the shrimp's back. A white or dark vein will be revealed. Try to put the tip of your knife under the vein and pull it out in one piece (or as much as one piece as possible) to get the cleanest removal. Some but not all have a vein on their underbelly too. Follow the same method there and you're done. Place the cleaned shrimp on a cool bed of ice and repeat. Now, my grandmother didn't throw anything away, so before you toss those shells in the can, consider this: you can make a nice, delicate seafood stock with them. Just add water, carrots, celery, and whatever herbs you like and boil them up to release their flavor. Strain and refrigerate for storage.

NOTES:

_____

_____

_____

_____

_____

_____

Crispy Corncob Corn Bread

I thought about changing the name of this recipe after so many geniuses kept asking me if they were really gonna eat a crispy corncob, but then I changed my mind. I mean, is everyone's mind so greased up with butter that they can't even hold a thought long enough to get it? I will never know, but what I do know is this is the best corn bread I've ever had and it's a great time to use that cast-iron skillet. Serve it up right at the table for a down-home feel.

Serves 6

1 tablespoon salted butter or bacon grease, plus more butter for serving

Kernels from 2 corncobs

1 cup Amy's Gluten-Free Mix

1 cup cornmeal (not too coarse)

1 tablespoon baking powder

2 tablespoons sugar

1 teaspoon salt

½ cup buttermilk

¼ cup milk

2 large eggs

2 tablespoons oil

Preheat the oven to 375°F.

In a 9-inch skillet over medium-high heat, melt the butter. When it foams up, add the corn and cook until the corn begins to brown. Remove from the heat and set aside.

In a nice big bowl, mix together the gluten-free mix, cornmeal, baking powder, sugar, and salt, and then add the buttermilk, milk, eggs, and oil. Stir until nice and thick. Add the roasted corn. Pour the batter back into the skillet and place it in the oven to bake until golden brown, about 20 minutes.

Slice and serve with some butter.

NOTES:

Repo Ron's Spareribs

We love to throw meat on the grill and cook it up because it gives us a chance to get caught up with the neighbors. Whenever Ronnie's grilling, our next-door neighbor is mowing. Somehow he ends up mowing our yard, too.

Serves 6

Salt and pepper

2 sides pork spareribs

1 jar Repo Ron's Sweet Lizard Lick Barbeque Sauce

Get the grill going nice and hot, and then get it down to a broil. Salt and pepper both sides of the ribs, and lay the ribs on the grill and broil for 20 minutes. Turn the ribs over and brush the ribs with Ronnie's barbeque sauce. Really slather it on. Cook the other side of the ribs for 20 minutes more, and then flip the ribs and slather more sauce on. Keep on doing this three or four more times, until the ribs are done.

Enjoy with my Anytime Coleslaw (page 85) and/or My Way Potato Salad (page 98).

Rib Tip: When preparing spareribs for the seasoning, grilling, and basting in their future, be sure to pull off the silverskin so all that sauce can do its job on the meat. If it hasn't already been removed by the butcher, you'll find that white membrane on the bony side of the rack. If you take care, you can grab it at the bone end and pull and work it off with your fingers, but slipping in a butter knife also does the trick.

NOTES:

_____

_____

_____

_____

Pecan-Crusted Pork Tenderloin

Tenderloins were meant to be crusted if you ask me. There's always a great ratio of meat to the crunchy seasoning, and the meat is kept super moist in the process. And when they are crusted with pecans on top of a good barbeque sauce, and then wrapped in bacon—well, you have a perfect way to end the day in the South.

Serves 4

1 cup chopped pecans

¾ teaspoon salt

½ teaspoon black pepper

½ teaspoon dried thyme

1 pound pork tenderloin

Barbeque Sauce (opposite page)

4 strips of bacon

Preheat the grill to hot.

Grind the pecans up with the salt, pepper, and thyme in a food processor. Dump the pecans on a nice big plate so you can roll the tenderloin in it.

Make little cuts in the tenderloin using just the tip of your knife. Slather the Barbeque Sauce all over the tenderloin, being sure it really gets into those little cuts. Next, roll the tenderloin in the pecans. Wrap the bacon tightly around the meat, sticking some toothpicks through the tenderloin to hold the bacon in place.

Slather with more sauce, and roast on the grill for 20 to 25 minutes, basting with more sauce all over the tenderloin as it cooks.

Remove from the grill and allow the tenderloin to rest for 5 minutes, wrapped in foil. Slice and serve.

NOTES:

_____

_____

_____

_____

_____

Barbeque Sauce

½ cup honey

¼ cup apple cider vinegar

3 tablespoons ketchup

2 tablespoons light brown
sugar

2 teaspoons gluten-free
Worcestershire sauce
(I like Lea & Perrins)

2 teaspoons hot sauce
(I like Frank's RedHot)

Salt and pepper to taste

In a medium bowl, mix all the ingredients, seasoning to taste.

NOTES:

_____

_____

_____

_____

_____

_____

Spoon Bread

You might not have ever had the pleasure, but in the South, spoon bread is about as important as biscuits. Dense and creamy, spoon bread is great all by itself with a slathering of butter right out of the oven or as a side to a hearty meat dish. It's been known to happen around our house that the spoon bread never makes it to the table because everyone gets after it like a bunch of turkey vultures the moment it comes out of the oven.

Serves 6

Salted butter for pan

1½ cups cornmeal

3 tablespoons Amy's Gluten-Free Mix

1¼ teaspoons salt

3 tablespoons sugar

2½ cups milk

4 tablespoons unsalted butter, melted

1 tablespoon sausage or bacon grease

4 large eggs

Preheat the oven to 375°F. Butter a 9 × 5 × 3-inch loaf pan and set aside.

In a nice big mixing bowl, stir together the cornmeal, gluten-free mix, salt, and sugar.

In a saucepan over medium heat, scald the milk, and then pour it into the dry ingredients, mixing until you can no longer see any dry bits.

Return the mixture to the saucepan and cook until the mixture looks like thick mush. Be sure to stir it the whole time so the dough doesn't stick to the bottom of the pan.

Stir in the melted butter, grease, and eggs. Mix until very thick, and then pour into your prepared pan.

Bake for 30 minutes, or until the top of the bread begins to brown just a bit.

Will keep, covered in the fridge, for a couple of days.

NOTES:

_____

_____

_____

_____

Three-Bean Salad

Three-bean salad is one of my favorite summer salads of all time. They say you can attract more flies with sugar than with vinegar, but since this recipe has the same amount of both, I'm still trying to figure that one out. Of course you can use fresh beans right out of the garden to make this recipe, but canned beans work just fine. Just remember not to stir it too much or the beans will break apart.

Serves 4

2 tablespoons red wine vinegar

2 tablespoons oil

2 tablespoons sugar

Salt and pepper to taste

1 (14.5-ounce) can wax beans

1 (14.5-ounce) can green beans

1 (14.5-ounce) can kidney beans

1 green onion, just the green parts

Salt and pepper to taste

Whisk together the vinegar, oil, and sugar. Season to taste with salt and pepper.

After you have drained and rinsed the beans, pour all of them into a medium-sized bowl. Drizzle the dressing over the beans and toss just a bit. Sprinkle the green onions over the top of the beans and serve. Now, how easy was that?

NOTES:

DESSERTS FOR THE SWEET TOOTH

I absolutely love sweets, but since my diagnosis, I can't tolerate sugar like I used to. That doesn't mean I can't enjoy some of my favorite treats every now and then; it just means I need to be mindful of what I'm eating and how much. Luckily nowadays we can substitute sweeteners like honey, coconut palm sugar, and dates for granulated white sugar. I've made suggestions as to possible substitutes for white sugar in some of the recipes, but modify as you see fit. When you are substituting coconut palm sugar, for example, it's the same amount as regular sugar—just be sure to grind it up good in a coffee grinder before using it. But when you use things like honey or maple syrup, you will need to be mindful of the amount of liquid you are adding. If you add more than ¼ cup of honey, for example, be sure to add 3 more tablespoons of my Gluten-Free Mix (page 26) so the recipe turns out just right. When you are using dates, you need to use more liquid so the recipe isn't too dry. When it comes to baking gluten-free, it's just like life: it's all about balance.

> **Women are like tea bags. You never know how strong they are until they are in hot water.**
> • • • • •
> **—Eleanor Roosevelt**

Some of my childhood favorites and some of the desserts my children (that includes you, Ronnie) love most contain marshmallows. I don't know about you, but I find it's pretty darn near impossible to replace a jet-puffed marshmallow with anything else, so you will see recipes for the whole sugar hog. Plus, I cook for others, not just myself, so I was adamant about including what other people in my life love in order to make the book a true reflection of what it means to be Amy Shirley.

Desserts

FOR THE SWEET TOOTH

Strawberry Cobbler

You can use fresh strawberries here, but frozen ones work just fine, too. More than anything, I love the texture of the fruit in this recipe! Adding the second half of the berries right before it bakes makes the filling turn almost into a chutney. Yum! If you're looking at that balsamic vinegar and wondering if I've lost my head, just trust me to steer you right. I swear it brings out the sweetness of the strawberries even more, and last I checked, my head's right on my shoulders where I left it.

Serves 6 to 8

**Unsalted butter
for greasing pan**

**1¾ cups Amy's
Gluten-Free Mix**

1 tablespoon baking powder

½ teaspoon salt

2 tablespoons sugar

**4 tablespoons shortening or
unsalted butter**

¾ cup half-and-half

Preheat the oven to 400°F. Butter a 14 × 10 × 2-inch roasting pan.

In a large mixing bowl, combine the gluten-free mix, baking powder, salt, and sugar. Add the shortening or the butter, and using your fingers, pinch the shortening or butter into the dry ingredients until you can no longer see clumps of fat.

Add the half-and-half, and mix just until combined. Set aside and make the filling.

FOR THE FILLING

½ cup granulated sugar

¼ cup firmly packed
light brown sugar

3 tablespoons cornstarch

Pinch of salt

6 cups strawberries,
frozen or fresh

2 tablespoons balsamic
vinegar

2 tablespoons unsalted butter

In a large bowl, mix the sugars, cornstarch, and salt together. Add the strawberries and the balsamic vinegar.

Melt the butter in a big pan and add 3 cups of the strawberries. Cook until they release their juices and the juices begin to thicken. Remove from the heat, and then stir in the remaining 3 cups of strawberries.

Pour into the prepared pan, and spoon the biscuit topping over the fruit.

Bake for 15 to 20 minutes, until the tops of the biscuits begin to brown.

Best served warm with ice cream or heavy cream.

Keeps like a champ for up to a week in the fridge.

NOTES:

_____

_____

_____

_____

_____

_____

1920 Miss American Pie

I named my lemon meringue pie the 1920 Miss American Pie in honor of the women's suffrage movement. Much like earning the right to vote was bittersweet, so is my pie.

Serves 6

½ recipe Golden Pie Crust (page 170)

1 cup plus 7 tablespoons sugar

3 tablespoons cornstarch

2 large eggs

4 large eggs, separated

⅓ cup lemon juice

Zest of 1 lemon

3 tablespoons salted butter

3 tablespoons unsalted butter

¼ teaspoon cream of tartar

½ teaspoon vanilla extract

Preheat the oven to 375°F.

Roll out your pie dough to ¼-inch thick, and line a 9-inch pie pan with it. Place it in the freezer while you make the filling.

In a large bowl, whisk 1 cup sugar and the cornstarch together, and then add the whole eggs and the egg yolks. Keep on beating those ingredients until the mixture is nice and pale looking. Add the lemon juice and zest and whisk until combined. Pour this mixture into a medium-sized saucepan, along with the salted and unsalted butter, and whisking the entire time, cook the filling over medium-low heat until it begins to thicken and coats the tines of the whisk.

Remove from the heat and pour into a cool bowl so the filling doesn't keep cookin'.

Now get that crust out of the freezer, line it with some parchment paper or foil, and then fill it with some pie weights like rice.

This is called blind baking. Place the crust in the oven and bake it for 20 minutes. Remove the crust from the oven and gingerly remove the pie weights and the paper or foil.

Reduce the heat of the oven to 350°F and keep baking the crust for 7 minutes more.

Now take that pie crust and pour the filling into it. Make it smooth so it bakes up right, and then put it back into the oven for 7 more minutes, until the filling is set.

Remove the pie from the oven, and then make your meringue.

In a large bowl, using a handheld mixer or a big fancy stand mixer, whip the egg whites until frothy. Add the cream of tartar and keep on beating the whites until soft peaks form. Beat in 7 tablespoons sugar and the vanilla extract, and whip for 1 minute.

Spread the meringue over the top of the pie, being sure to seal it with the crust.

Return the pie to the oven and bake for 5 to 10 minutes, until the meringue is golden brown.

Meringue Tips: If you're feeling at all unsure of yourself when it comes to making meringue, let me ease your fears. Meringues look fancy, but they're really simple. All you're doing is whisking some air into the egg whites, much like you do when you're whipping cream. Egg whites just do it with more foam and flair. I'll tell you a few secrets: Big and fluffy meringue works best with eggs that are a few days old. Always use room-temperature eggs for the best volume. And if you try to make meringue on a rainy day, you're setting yourself up for failure. The humidity can really put a damper on those bubbles you're trying to set up!

NOTES:

Golden Pie Crust

**Makes enough pastry
for a double-crust pie**

¾ cup (1½ sticks)
unsalted butter

2 cups Amy's Gluten-Free Mix

1 tablespoon sugar

¼ teaspoon salt

1 large egg yolk

1 large egg

Real easy, y'all. I like to use my mixer for this one, but you can use a pastry cutter or even your hands. If you are going rogue and just using your hands, move fast because your hands are hot and will make the dough get soft. Using your mixer with the paddle attachment, add the butter to the flour mix, along with the sugar and the salt. Mix on low until you can't see any lumps of butter anymore. Add the egg yolk and the egg, and mix until the dough comes together in a big sticky ball. Turn the dough onto a counter lightly dusted with more mix, and knead with the palm of your hand until nice and smooth. (Remember, if you overmix the dough it will be too soft to knead; just put it in the fridge if this happens.) Wrap the dough in plastic wrap and chill it out in the fridge for at least a couple of hours.

Freezes great for up to 2 months and stays fresh in the fridge for 3 days.

NOTES:

_____

_____

_____

_____

_____

Chess Pie

When I was little, I thought this was called the Chest Pie. I didn't realize I heard wrong until one day after church I was bragging on my mom's Chest Pie and someone said, "Chest pie? I've never heard of that before! Does it have sunken treasure in it?" Ha! I told them yes it did because my mama made it, but then I got my facts straight real quick so I wouldn't get licked again.

Serves 9 because it's rich

½ recipe Golden Pie Crust (opposite page)

6 egg yolks

¾ cup granulated sugar

1 cup firmly packed light brown sugar

1 tablespoon Amy's Gluten-Free Mix

½ cup salted butter, melted

½ cup milk

¼ cup evaporated milk

1 tablespoon vanilla extract

Preheat the oven to 375°F. Roll out your pie dough to ¼ inch thick, and line a 9-inch pie pan with it. Place it in the freezer while you make the filling.

In a large bowl, whisk together the yolks and the granulated sugar with ¼ cup of the light brown sugar until light. In another bowl, mix together the remaining light brown sugar with my gluten-free mix. Add the melted butter to the flour and sugar mixture. Now add the egg yolks to the flour mixture and mix until smooth. Add the milk, evaporated milk, and vanilla extract, and then pour the mixture into the unbaked pie crust. Bake for 20 to 30 minutes, until the center is set.

Allow to cool until you are ready to serve.

NOTES:

Banana Puddin'

I won't lie: there are a couple things that post-diagnosis were extremely hard to come to terms with not ever having again. Have I mentioned that I am a big sweets person? Honestly my favorite food of all time prior to being diagnosed was banana pudding. I confess it took me a long, long time to try to make this gluten-free, probably because I feared it wouldn't hold up to my expectations. So here it is, another dish that helped me see the light in my completely gluten-free life. You can use gluten-free vanilla wafers and a meringue topping like my mama does to gussy up your Banana Puddin', but crumbs from my vanilla sheet cake work just as well, and I made it easy on you with some cream in a can for a topping.

Serves 6

½ cup sugar

¼ teaspoon salt

3 tablespoons cornstarch

4 large egg yolks

2 large whole eggs

2 cups half-and-half

2 teaspoons vanilla extract

2 tablespoons unsalted butter

2 cups crumbled 1-2-3-4 Cake (page 195)

2 super ripe bananas, sliced

Reddi-wip or other whipped cream, for serving

In a large bowl, whisk the sugar and salt with the cornstarch, and then add the egg yolks and the whole eggs. Whisk this until the mixture gets really fluffy and pale, like a Sunday morning.

Heat the half-and-half on the stove in a good-sized saucepan just until it steams. Pour this hot cream into the eggs, whisking that egg mixture the whole time so you don't end up with sweet scrambled eggs. Pour this mixture back into the pan, and then whisking the whole time (and I mean the whole time), cook this puddin' over medium heat. When it gets thick, remove it from the stove and stir in the vanilla extract and the butter.

Crumble up the leftover cake into a nice big bowl so you don't mess up the whole counter, and then start putting everything together. First do a layer of the puddin' in a nice clear glass bowl or pudding cups, then a layer of bananas, and then a layer of crumbs. Repeat this until all the puddin' is used up and you're out of bananas.

Top the pudding with some whipped cream—you know, like Reddi-wip or something else out of a can.

Place in the fridge overnight so it's icebox cold the next day (when it tastes the best as far as I'm concerned). Keeps for a week.

NOTES:

_____

_____

_____

_____

_____

_____

Peanut Butter Pie

I love me some peanut butter, and I really love this pie because it's not too sweet. Sometimes when I'm feeling extra healthy, I like to use coconut palm sugar instead of the light brown sugar or the regular sugar. It's got this almost molasses-ey flavor that goes just right with the peanut butter, and it's low glycemic!

Serves 6

1 (8-ounce) package cream cheese, at room temperature

1¼ cups creamy peanut butter (I like Jif)

¼ cup firmly packed light brown sugar

¼ cup granulated sugar

¼ teaspoon salt

¼ teaspoon vanilla extract

1 chocolate cookie crust (see Grasshopper Pie, page 176)

1 (12-ounce) tub of Cool Whip, thawed

Semisweet chocolate for grating

In a large bowl using a handheld mixer, mix the cream cheese, peanut butter, brown sugar, granulated sugar, salt, and vanilla extract until creamy.

Pour the filling into your prepared pie crust. Smooth the top, and then stir the Cool Whip until creamy. Spread it over the peanut butter filling.

Refrigerate until ready to serve.

Grate a little chocolate over the top of the pie for a pretty look.

NOTES:

Cherries Jubilee

The only thing you need to be careful about when you are making this recipe is not to wear too much hair spray so you don't burst into flames. If you really want to get theatrical with this one, turn the dining room lights down low (but not off—you need to be able to see what's in front of you!) and walk in when the cherries are lit. You can then serve them up tableside like they do it in old-school restaurants. Just scoop the ice cream into bowls beforehand, then scoop the flambéed cherries and syrup over the top and sprinkle on those almonds.

Serves 4 to 6

1 cup sugar

½ cup water

2 pounds Bing cherries, washed and pitted (frozen work fine)

¼ cup cherry brandy (kirsch)

⅓ cup cognac (or an additional ⅓ cup brandy)

2 cups vanilla ice cream

½ cup sliced almonds for serving

Pour the sugar into a medium-sized saucepan with the water, and heat over medium-high heat until the sugar has melted. Add the cherries and heat just until the cherries are warm. Remove from the heat. Add the brandy and allow to sit for 15 minutes.

Using a strainer, drain the syrup into a bowl, then pour the syrup back into the saucepan and set aside.

Scoop the cherries out of the strainer and into a second pan over medium heat. Add the fancy cognac (or more brandy), and bring to a simmer. Remove the pan from the heat. Using a long-necked lighter or match, ignite the cherries.

When the flame has died down, spoon out some of the cherries over a scoop of the ice cream. Drizzle some of the reserved syrup over the whole thing, and then sprinkle the ice cream with the almonds.

NOTES:

_____

_____

_____

_____

Grasshopper Pie

I know that Grasshopper Pie isn't the most famous pie in the world, but I love how it's like a giant Andes mint. I'd always grab those mints by the handful when we'd leave any restaurant. They were like shiny little green gift-wrapped packages. I still think they are the most refreshing mints after a good supper, just like this pie. I use a gluten-free chocolate wafer cookie to make the pie shell here, which can be used in any number of pie recipes or even as the base for a cheesecake.

Serves 6

14 Glutino or Kinnikinnick chocolate cream cookies

5 tablespoons unsalted butter, melted

24 large marshmallows

½ cup milk

4 tablespoons green crème de menthe

2 tablespoons white crème de cacao

Green food coloring (optional)

1 cup heavy cream

Remove the cream filling from the cookies using the flat side of a knife. Place all the cookies in a medium-sized bowl or a food processor, and crush the cookies until almost a powder. Pour the melted butter over the cookie crumbs and stir together. Press the mixture into the bottom and sides of a 9-inch pie pan to create a pie shell.

In a glass bowl in the microwave, melt the marshmallows in the milk. Add the crème de menthe, crème de cacao, and a few drops of green food coloring if you want a nice pop of color. Chill for 10 minutes. Meanwhile, in a separate bowl, whip the cream until it holds firm folds.

Fold the whipped cream into the marshmallow mixture. Pour into the shell and freeze. Serve icebox cold.

NOTES:

_____

_____

_____

_____

_____

_____

Gluten-Free Butterscotch Crimpets

I made these because I had Tastykake Butterscotch Krimpets pretty much whenever I could when I was a little girl. The truck stop by my house always had fresh ones, and I've gotta tell ya, these taste just like 'em.

Makes 24

**Unsalted butter
for greasing pan**

**4 large eggs, at room
temperature**

1 cup granulated sugar

**1 cup firmly packed
light brown sugar**

1 tablespoon vanilla extract

½ cup milk

½ cup evaporated milk

2 tablespoons unsalted butter

2 cups Amy's Gluten-Free Mix

1 teaspoon baking powder

½ teaspoon salt

FOR THE ICING

**⅓ cup gluten-free
butterscotch chips**

**½ cup unsalted butter,
at room temperature**

1¾ cups confectioners' sugar

**2 tablespoons
evaporated milk**

1 teaspoon vanilla extract

¼ teaspoon salt

Preheat the oven to 350°F. Lightly grease a jelly roll pan with butter, and then line it with parchment paper.

In a large bowl with a handheld mixer, whip the eggs with the granulated sugar and the light brown sugar until light and fluffy. Add the vanilla extract and whip until very smooth.

Warm the milk and evaporated milk in the microwave with the butter for 30 seconds. Remove and heat again for 15 seconds to make sure the butter is melted.

Sift the gluten-free mix, baking powder, and salt into the whipped eggs. Fold the dry ingredients into the eggs, and then add the milk and butter in a slow steady stream while you continue to mix the batter.

Pour the batter into your prepared jelly roll pan, and bake for 20 to 25 minutes.

While the cake is baking, whip up the icing. In a medium glass bowl, melt the butterscotch chips and the butter in the microwave. Stir until smooth. Add the confectioners' sugar, evaporated milk, vanilla extract, and salt.

Pour the icing over the warm cake, and then smooth the surface. Cut into 24 pieces and serve.

NOTES:

Honey Dew Cookies

Nothing says easy like a spoonful of honey. Even better? These cookies can be made with chilled coconut oil or Crisco if you don't want the butter. Now everyone can be happy, no matter what you can't eat.

Makes 24 cookies

6 tablespoons unsalted butter

½ cup honey

¼ cup sugar

1 large egg

2⅓ cups Amy's Gluten-Free Mix, plus additional mix or tapioca starch for flouring work surface

¼ teaspoon salt

1 teaspoon baking soda

Preheat the oven to 350°F. Line two cookie sheets with parchment paper.

In the large bowl of a stand-up mixer, whip the butter until nice and soft. Beat in the honey and the sugar, and then add the egg and mix until very smooth. Gradually add the gluten-free mix, salt, and baking soda, and mix until the dough comes together. Refrigerate for 2 to 4 hours.

Roll the dough into a log on a surface that has been lightly floured with either more of my mix or some tapioca starch. Then roll the dough out until it's ¼ inch thick. Cut the cookies with a 2-inch round cutter and place on the cookie sheet, about 2 inches apart.

Bake for 8 to 10 minutes. Remove from the oven. Let cool on the sheets for 5 minutes, and then move to wire racks to finish cooling.

Keep perfectly in a cookie tin for up to a week.

NOTES:

_____

_____

_____

_____

_____

_____

Root Beer Float

Grab some straws and an old soda fountain glass for an extra-special trip down memory lane, just with way different clothes on.

Serves 1 to 2
(if you feel like sharing)

1 pint dairy-free ice cream (I like NadaMoo!)

1 can gluten-free root beer (I like Maine Root)

Put two scoops of the dairy-free ice cream in a big glass, and then pour the root beer over the top and watch it fizz and foam, fizz and foam. Serve with a spoon and a bendy striped straw, two if you're sharing. Now swing your legs like you're sitting on the stool at the soda counter.

Never keeps longer than 15 minutes.

NOTES:

_____
_____
_____
_____
_____
_____

People are like stained glass windows. They sparkle and shine when the sun is out, but when the darkness sets in, their true beauty is revealed only if there is a light from within.

—Elisabeth Kübler-Ross

Lizard Limelight Atlantic Beach Pie

When I have time to read, I like to read all kinds of things, but when I read Bill Smith's recipe for Atlantic Beach Lemon-Lime Pie, my eyelashes curled a little tighter, I got so wound up with wanting it. I could tell he might have key lime pie beat in my book. Now this might seem like a fancy pie, what with the sea salt and all, but let's just remember we are talking about salt here. And guess what? This pie will make you feel like a million bucks.

Serves 8

FOR THE CRUST

4 (4.4-ounce) bags (1¾ cups) gluten-free table crackers (I like Glutino)

¼ cup sugar

1½ teaspoons sea salt (fancy!)

6 tablespoons unsalted butter, softened

FOR THE FILLING

1 (14-ounce) can sweetened condensed milk

4 large egg yolks

¼ cup lemon juice

¼ cup lime juice

1 cup heavy cream

¼ cup sugar

Coarse sea salt for garnish

Preheat the oven to 350°F.

Take a rolling pin and gently whack those bags of crackers until they're all broken up good. I like a few big bits to remain for a nice texture. If this feels too violent, just use your hands to crush the crackers in a nice big pan.

Add the sugar and the sea salt, and then using your fingers, cut the butter into the crackers until it starts to hold together. Press the crust into an 8-inch pie pan and bake for 15 minutes, just until the crust has a little tan.

While that is in the oven, in the large bowl of a stand-up mixer, whisk together the condensed milk and the egg yolks until super smooth and you can't see any more streaks of yellow. Add the lemon and lime juices, and mix very well.

When the pie crust is done, remove it from the oven, and then pour the filling into it. Return to the oven and bake for 16 minutes more. Remove from the oven, allow the pie to cool completely, and then refrigerate so the pie becomes icebox cold.

In a large bowl, whip the cream with the sugar until it holds firm folds.

Serve each slice of pie with a generous scoop of the cream and some sea salt sprinkled on top. This pie keeps for 4 days in the fridge.

NOTES:

Maggie's Red Velvet Cake

My daughter Maggie's favorite cake is by far the red velvet, so I had to make sure she could make it gluten-free. Luckier than a three-legged dog in hubcap factory, I was able to pull it off. If you'd prefer to make red velvet cupcakes so that everybody gets their own, be my guest. Just reduce the cooking time down to 15 to 20 minutes.

Serves 8

Unsalted butter
for greasing pans

11 tablespoons
unsalted butter

1½ cups sugar

3 large eggs

2¼ cups Amy's
Gluten-Free Mix

2 tablespoons unsweetened
cocoa powder

1½ teaspoons baking powder

½ teaspoon baking soda

½ teaspoon salt

1 teaspoon white vinegar

1 tablespoon vanilla extract

1 cup buttermilk

7 to 8 drops red food coloring

Cream Cheese Frosting
(opposite page)

Preheat the oven to 350°F. Grease two 8-inch round cake pans with butter. Line the bottom of the pans with waxed paper or parchment.

In a large bowl with a handheld mixer, cream together the butter and the sugar until light and fluffy.

Add the eggs, and beat on high for 3 minutes, until the eggs are nice and fluffy. Sift together the gluten-free mix, cocoa powder, baking powder, baking soda, and salt. In three batches, add the flour to the butter and egg mixture. Mix on high after each addition. Add the vinegar, vanilla extract, and buttermilk. Mix just until incorporated. Add the food coloring and mix until you can no longer see any red streaks.

Divide the batter between the two pans and bake for 25 to 30 minutes, rotating the pans halfway through for a nice even bake.

Allow the cakes to cool in the pan for 15 minutes, and then invert onto a wire rack to cool completely.

Meanwhile, make my famous Cream Cheese Frosting.

To assemble the cake, place one cake layer on a plate and ice just the top of the cake with a generous helping of the icing. Top with the other cake layer, and then ice with a light coating of the icing all over the cake. Place the cake in the freezer for 10 minutes, and then ice the cake with the rest of the icing.

Will keep on the counter until ready to serve, or store in the fridge for up to a week.

Cream Cheese Frosting

6 tablespoons unsalted butter, at room temperature

2 (8-ounce) packages cream cheese, at room temperature

2 cups confectioners' sugar

Grated zest from 1 lemon

Using a handheld mixer and a nice big bowl, cream the butter until it is silky smooth. Add the cream cheese and mix until smooth. Add the sugar and the lemon zest, and mix until light and fluffy.

NOTES:

_____

_____

_____

_____

_____

_____

If you go around watching every word you say all the time, you'll never get much said.

—Lucy van Pelt

Mississippi Mud Bars

I may not be able to eat chocolate all the time, but I sure do know a lot of chocolate lovers. My kids go crazy for these bars, and when I was little, boy howdy, I sure did too. You can make the base all by itself for some rich, warm brownies if you are in a hurry or just need something to bring to a friend's house when you are out of Lemon Poppy Seed Friendship Muffins (page 44).

Serves 16

Nonstick cooking spray

2 sticks unsalted butter

4 ounces unsweetened chocolate

1½ cups granulated sugar

½ cup firmly packed dark brown sugar

3 large eggs

1 tablespoon vanilla extract

1½ cups Amy's Gluten-Free Mix

½ teaspoon baking soda

¾ teaspoon salt

3 cups miniature marshmallows

Preheat the oven to 350°F. Line a 13 × 9 × 2-inch pan with aluminum foil, using enough so there is a 1-inch overhang. Spray the foil with nonstick cooking spray.

In a large saucepan, melt the butter with the chocolate over low heat. When it is silky smooth, stir in the granulated sugar and dark brown sugar. Whisk in the eggs and the vanilla extract. Add the gluten-free mix, baking soda, and salt.

Pour the batter into the prepared pan and spread it out evenly.

Bake for 30 minutes, rotating the pan halfway through. After 30 minutes, remove the pan from the oven, add the marshmallows, and bake for 10 minutes more.

FOR THE ICING

½ cup (1 stick) unsalted butter

2 cups confectioners' sugar

½ cup cocoa powder

¼ cup evaporated milk

⅓ cup chopped pecans

While the bars are finishing up in the oven, make the easy caramel icing. In a medium-sized saucepan over low heat, melt the butter, and then stir in the confectioners' sugar and cocoa powder. Whisk in the evaporated milk, remove the pan from the heat, and let the icing sit and thicken up until you are ready to pour it over the bars.

Stir the chopped pecans into the icing right before you pour it over the marshmallows for the best result. Once the bars are done baking, pour the icing over the marshmallows. Let the bars cool and the icing set a bit before slicing into 16 pieces.

These bars keep for up to a week.

NOTES:

Orange Upside-Down Picnic Cake

One of my formerly favorite things that I will never ever be allowed to eat again (I have a bad reaction to pineapple) is what a lot of people call a picnic cake or upside-down cake. For that recipe, you soak the cake with pineapple juice and caramelize the pineapple slices that decorate the top of the cake. I thought I was resigned to not ever having that sort of pleasure again, but then I realized there's no harm in trying to make something just as good. That's how this Orange Upside-Down Picnic Cake came into being, and I tell ya, between this and my banana puddin', I know I'm onto something here. You can use the mandarin oranges out of a can or you can peel them fresh. Either way, this cake sure is delicious and travels like a champ, making it the perfect thing to pack up in the car and go.

Serves 8

Unsalted butter for greasing pan

1½ cups sugar

½ cup water

1 (24-ounce) can mandarin orange segments, or 4 mandarin oranges, peeled and segmented

6 tablespoons unsalted butter

Zest of 2 mandarin oranges or 1 orange

3 large eggs

1½ cups Amy's Gluten-Free Mix

1⅛ teaspoons baking powder

¼ teaspoon salt

¾ cup milk

¼ teaspoon vanilla extract

Preheat the oven to 350°F. Butter an 8-inch square pan with unsalted butter and set aside. This step is important, so don't skip it. If you don't butter it, the oranges will stick to the pan—ruining your cake.

In a saucepan over high heat, dissolve ½ cup sugar in the water and boil it until it begins to take on a light to medium brown color, about 8 to 10 minutes.

Line the mandarin orange segments in the bottom of your prepared pan. Pour the caramelized sugar over the oranges so that they are covered.

In the large bowl of a stand-up mixer with a paddle attachment, cream the butter with 1 cup sugar and the zest. Scrape down the sides of the bowl so you don't have a layer of unwhipped butter on your hands. When the butter is pale and fluffy, add the eggs and whip on high until very light and fluffy. Add the gluten-free mix, baking powder, and salt, and mix on low. Add the milk and vanilla extract, and mix on high until the batter is light and fluffy.

Pour the batter over the orange segments, and bake for 25 to 30 minutes, until the cake is golden brown and a toothpick comes out clean.

Let the cake cool for 10 minutes, run a knife around the edge of the pan, and then invert the cake onto a serving platter.

Keeps on the counter for a week. Seriously.

NOTES:

_____

_____

_____

_____

_____

_____

Peachy Keen Slump

Peaches from the Carolinas are as juicy as the day is long and I prefer a slump to a cobbler because the dumplings are as creamy as a steamed pudding. To top it off, you can drown your warm servings of slump in thick, cool cream for a tangy treat.

Serves 6

FOR THE FILLING

½ cup firmly packed light brown sugar

¾ cup granulated sugar

1½ teaspoons fresh ginger, minced, or ¾ teaspoon ground ginger

3 tablespoons cornstarch

¼ teaspoon salt

4 cups peeled and sliced peaches (frozen peach slices work just as well; just defrost them first)

2 tablespoons unsalted butter

3 tablespoons bourbon

FOR THE DUMPLINGS

1½ cups Amy's Gluten-Free Mix

⅔ cup sugar

1 teaspoon baking powder

¼ teaspoon salt

4 tablespoons unsalted butter, diced

Preheat the oven to 375°F.

In a big ol' mixing bowl, mix together the sugars for the filling along with the ginger, cornstarch, and salt. Add the peaches and toss to cover them real good. Melt the butter in a large oven-safe pot over medium-high heat. Add the peaches and stir them around so they won't stick. Reduce the heat to medium-low and cook, stirring every once in a while. When the peaches get nice and thick, add the bourbon and stir just to combine. Cook the mixture a little longer until it thickens up. Remove from the heat.

For the dumplings, combine the gluten-free mix, sugar, baking powder, and salt, and then add the butter. Using the fingers the Lord gave you, roll the butter in the flour until the mixture looks like damp sugar. Add the eggs and the milk, and stir with a spoon until it begins to thicken up.

Let the batter sit for 5 minutes. Then drop the dough by table-spoonfuls in the pot, leaving spaces between the balls of dough.

Return the pot to the stove and heat until it boils. Cover the slump with a tight-fitting lid and reduce the heat to simmer. Cook on the stove for 20 minutes, and then transfer to your hot oven and bake for 15 minutes. Remove the lid from the pot and bake for another 10 minutes to brown the dumplings.

2 large eggs

¼ cup milk

Heavy cream or vanilla ice cream, for serving

Serve hot with heavy cream or ice cream, whichever you prefer. I don't do too much dairy, so I often just eat mine plain or with dairy-free ice cream and it's still all good.

Stays pretty as a picture for a week in the fridge.

NOTES:

_____

_____

_____

_____

_____

_____

Pepsi Peanut Pie

Who needs corn syrup when you can make your own with a can of Pepsi? I simply love this pie because it's so salty and sweet at the same time. And yes, Pepsi is gluten-free. The caramel color they use isn't made from wheat, barley, or rye, which isn't always the case with dark-colored sodas.

Serves 8

½ recipe Golden Pie Crust (page 170)

2 large eggs

½ cup creamy peanut butter (I like Jif)

⅔ cup firmly packed light brown sugar

1 tablespoon cornmeal

1 tablespoon Amy's Gluten-Free Mix

4 tablespoons unsalted butter, melted

¾ cup Pepsi Syrup (opposite page)

2 teaspoons vanilla extract

1¼ cups roasted salted peanuts

Preheat the oven to 350°F. Roll out your pie dough to ¼ inch thick and line a 9-inch pie pan with it. Place it in the freezer while you make the filling.

In a large bowl using a hand mixer, whip the eggs until they look totally mixed and pale yellow. Add the peanut butter and mix until totally incorporated. Then add the light brown sugar and mix until totally combined. Next goes in the cornmeal and the gluten-free mix, again being sure to mix until you can't see the dry ingredients. Add the melted butter, Pepsi Syrup, and vanilla extract. Mix until the mixture looks like a nice smooth batter. Fold in the salted peanuts.

Pour the filling into the prepared pie pan. Bake for 40 minutes, until the center of the pie is set.

Remove from the oven and allow to cool completely. I like to put my pie in the fridge for 20 minutes just before I serve it so it slices up real nice.

I kid you not, you can keep this pie on the counter or in the fridge—it tastes delicious up to a week of keepin' it.

NOTES:

_____

_____

_____

_____

Pepsi Syrup

1½ cups sugar

½ teaspoon cream of tartar

⅛ teaspoon salt

1½ cups Pepsi

Combine the sugar, cream of tartar, salt, and Pepsi in a medium saucepan over medium-high heat. Whisking the whole time, bring the syrup to a boil. Then reduce the heat to a simmer. Cover the pot with a lid and simmer for 4 minutes. Remove the lid and keep cooking the syrup down until it reduces and begins to foam. Remove from the heat. Set aside to cool.

NOTES:

Sun Tea Cake

There ain't nothing more southern than a glass of ice tea on a hot Carolina day, so when I'm making my tea out on my back porch, I've always got another mason jar filled with butter and a tea bag so I can make this cake. But don't worry; if you are in a hurry, you can use what I call my quick sunbeam for a minute or two—that would be the microwave.

Serves 6 to 8

**Unsalted butter
for greasing pan**

½ cup sliced almonds, skin on

**1 cup (2 sticks)
unsalted butter, melted**

2 Lipton Iced Tea bags

Zest of 1 lemon

¼ teaspoon ground nutmeg

Splash of vanilla extract

**4 large eggs,
at room temperature**

**2 large egg yolks,
at room temperature**

1 cup sugar

**1½ cup Amy's
Gluten-Free Mix**

3 tablespoons cornstarch

Heaping ¼ teaspoon salt

Preheat the oven to 350°F. Butter a 9-inch tube pan. Spread the sliced almonds over the bottom of the pan.

Place the butter and the tea bags in a large mason jar and set it out on the back porch to melt in the sun. The tea will flavor the butter, so the longer you leave it out there, the stronger the tea taste will be. I like to leave mine out there for about 30 minutes after the butter has melted completely for a delicate tea flavor and longer for the hit-you-over-the-head kind of taste.

Then bring the butter back inside and discard the tea bags, squeezing the liquid from the bags before you toss them. Add the lemon zest to the butter along with the nutmeg and the splash of vanilla (really just a little—not a big splash, a little splash).

Now, in a large mixing bowl with a handheld mixer, whip the eggs, the yolks, and the sugar until the eggs triple in volume.

Sift the gluten-free mix and cornstarch over the eggs, and then drizzle in the butter. Fold the dry ingredients in along with the salt, just enough that you can't see the dry ingredients anymore.

Pour the batter into the pan and bake for 45 minutes, until the cake is golden and has begun to pull away from the sides of the pan.

Let the cake cool in the pan for 20 minutes. Run a butter knife around the edge of the cake to separate it from the pan. Invert the tube pan over a wire rack or, if you are a rebel like me, over your serving platter. I like to press just a little bit on the bottom of the tube pan and maybe drum a little tune and the cake will release. The almonds should look real nice.

NOTES:

_____

_____

_____

_____

_____

_____

Sunday Service Moonshine Pound Cake

I was told moonshine was best when it was made on a Sunday, so why not make a pound cake with it if you ain't drinking it? Since Ronnie and I aren't big drinkers, I wouldn't know either way, but I can appreciate someone who is good at what he or she does. Popcorn Sutton was a legendary moonshine maker who is no longer with us, but if he was, I would be sure to send him one of these pound cakes. If you're a purist and you like your pound cake plain and simple, maybe with a cup of tea, this one will rise to that occasion. Just omit the moonshine and you're as ready to roll as Ronnie before a repo. But I've gotta say, this pound cake lends itself just as well to a scoop of ice cream and toasted pecans or a handful of berries and whipped cream, so don't limit yourself whatever you do. I'd even grill ripe Carolina peaches and top a slice of this cake with them. Now you've gone and given me some ideas.

Makes 1 loaf

**Unsalted butter
for greasing pan**

1 cup unsalted butter

1 cup sugar

6 large eggs

**2 cups Amy's Gluten-Free
Flour Mix, sifted**

1 teaspoon salt

¼ teaspoon baking soda

2 tablespoons vanilla extract

**2 tablespoons moonshine
(I like Popcorn Sutton's
Tennessee White Whiskey)**

Preheat the oven to 325°F. Grease a 9 × 5 × 3-inch loaf pan with butter and line the bottom with waxed paper or parchment paper.

In the large bowl of a stand-up mixer with a paddle attachment or with a hand mixer, beat the butter with the sugar until nice and pale. Add the eggs one at a time and mix until the eggs double in size.

Sift the gluten-free mix a couple of times and then add to the egg mixture. Mix on high for 1 minute. Add the salt and baking soda, and then the vanilla extract and moonshine.

Pour the batter into the prepared pan and bake for 1 hour, or until a toothpick comes out clean.

Allow to cool in the pan for 10 minutes before inverting onto a wire rack to cool completely.

Keeps perfect as a Christmas present for up to a week (wrapped up like a newborn, of course!).

NOTES:

The 1-2-3-4 Cake

This cake is about as classic as they come. Speaking of legends, it has been around longer than Popcorn Sutton's moonshine and was the first cake my mama taught me how to make. Everybody needs one of these in their repertoire. How else can they ever make anyone they love a layered birthday cake? The fact that it was the first cake I made gluten-free after my diagnosis makes it that much more special. It made gluten-free as easy as 1-2-3-4 for me—as it will for you.

Serves 6

Unsalted butter
for greasing pans

1 cup unsalted butter

2 cups sugar

4 large eggs

3 cups Amy's Gluten-Free Mix

4 teaspoons baking powder

½ teaspoon salt

1 cup milk

2 tablespoons vanilla extract

Amy's Buttercream Icing
(page 10)

Preheat the oven to 350°F. Grease two 9-inch round cake pans with unsalted butter and line with parchment paper on the bottom.

In the large bowl of a stand-up mixer with a paddle attachment, whip the butter with the sugar. Add the eggs and whip until light and fluffy. Next add the gluten-free mix, baking powder, salt, milk, and vanilla extract. Mix on high until nice and smooth.

Divide the batter between the two pans and bake for 20 to 25 minutes, rotating the pans halfway through, from top to bottom, so they bake evenly.

Allow to cool in the pan for 10 minutes, and then invert onto a wire rack to finish cooling off.

Now make my Buttercream Icing. After the cakes have cooled, place one cake round on a plate or stand. Ice just the top of the cake. Add the other cake round top side down, and then ice the rest of the cake. Slice and serve!

NOTES:

_____

_____

_____

_____

Acknowledgments

Being that I am gooder than grits and not half as dusty most days, I know that I would not be the person I am today without help. So I would like to start by thanking the one who has never left my side and has kept me between the ditch, and that is the Good Lord Above!

Of course throughout my childhood, my mother was a rock. She may have allowed me to fall but she was always there to pick me back up.

To my two older sisters, Donna and Nancy, I would not have ya'll any other way. Our love will remain to the end of time.

To Brandy, April, and Bubba, my taste testers, thanks for at least trying my gluten-free food. Ha.

To the one in my life, who never ceases to amaze me, supports me, allows me to be a superhero, because in the end it is us against the world, I love you, my best friend—Ronnie Shackles Shirley!

Alexa, Alex, Gabe, and Maggie, you all are my heart. I pray as a mother that I live to see you make your dreams come true! Thank you for just being your loving, outgoing, joking, kid selves.

To Nana and Pops (Ronnie's parents), thank you for all the Sunday dinners and the love and acceptance when I entered your family.

For the ones like my grandmother and my papa that look down from heaven, I pray that I have made you proud. Love you.

To my friend Karen, thank you for taking the time to help someone in need. Words cannot express what you have done for me, but I pray this book will help others as you helped me. Thank you with all my heart.

Lastly, to HarperOne, thank you for taking a chance on a gluten-free, country-posh gal from North Carolina.

LIST OF RESOURCES

My list of gluten-free brands and products you can live by (and on):

Rickland Organics™ Crispy Treats

Lärabar®

KIND® Bars

BumbleBars®

Pacific Gold Beef Jerky®

The Better Chip®

Garden Veggie Straws®

Kirkland Signature™ Organic
Tortilla Strips

Kirkland Signature™ Kettle® Brand
Potato Chips

Snikiddy® Veggie Chips

Pirate's Booty®

Food Should Taste Good™

Kirkland Signature™
Microwave Popcorn

Angie's Kettle Corn

Beanitos®

Kellogg's® Fruity Snacks

Fruit by the Foot®

Welch's Fruit Snacks

Stretch Island® Fruit Co.

180 Snacks®

Go Raw

Kirkland Signature™
Cashew Clusters

Clif Kid™ Organic Z Fruit™ Rope

YumEarth® Organics

Bare Fruit® Apple Chips

Kirkland Signature™ Super
Extra-Large Peanuts

Wonderful® Pistachios

Popchips®

CytoSport™ Whey Protein

Nature Nate's Natural™ Honey

Kirkland Signature™ Clover Honey

Mamma Chia®

GoGo squeeZ™

MaraNatha® Almond Butter

Jif®

Made in Nature™

Ocean Spray® Craisins®

Mariani® Paradise Isle Tropical Fruit Blend

Philippine Brand™ Dried Young Coconut

Mary's Gone Crackers®

Nature's Earthly Choice™ Quinoa

Classico® Tomato and Basil Pasta Sauce

Ancient Harvest® Pasta

Premium Gold® Flaxseed

Spam®

Tasty Bite® Madras Lentils™

Stagg Chili®

Calrose Rice

Mori-nu® Tofu

Kirkland Signature™ Organic Chicken Stock

Lundberg Rice

Idahoan® Instant Potatoes

Hungry Jack® Instant Potatoes

Lindsay Olives

Ro-Tel®

Cholula® Hot Sauce

TABASCO® Sauce

Mateo's Gourmet Salsa

505 Southwestern® Roasted Green Chiles

Heinz® Ketchup

Lea & Perrins® Worcestershire Sauce

Paisley Farm Bean Salad

Tassos® Olives

Stubb's® BBQ Sauce

Carrington Farms Coconut Oil

Hellmann's® Mayonnaise

Krusteaz® Brownie Mix

Arm & Hammer® Baking Soda

Wholesome® Sweeteners (cane sugar and agave nectar)

Imperial® Sugar

Honeyville® Almond Flour

Heinz® Vinegar

Nestlé® Carnation® Evaporated Milk

Kirkland Signature™ Organic Ricemilk

Blue Diamond® Almond Breeze® Almondmilk

Kirkland Signature™ Greek Yogurt

Hebrew National® Hot Dogs

Kirkland Signature™ Beef Dogs

Kirkland Signature™
Sliced Turkey Breast

Kirkland Signature™
Turkey Burgers

Cedarlane® Veggie & Grain Bowl

Skotidakis™ Greek Yogurt Dip

Leigh Oliver's™ White Queso

La Terra Fina® Dip

Hail Merry®

GoodFoods™ Tableside
Guacamole

Nuovo Ravioli

Jones Canadian Bacon

Columbus® Meats

Lowes Foods Sausages

Now, you remember when I told you that Karen sent me a list of gluten-free products I could start buying right away to replace all the big stuff? Well, here are all the products she led me to. All of these can be found at Whole Foods and other natural food stores

Bob's Red Mill® Flours

Arrowhead Mills® Flours

Ian's® Frozen Chicken Nuggets

Smart Flour™ Foods Frozen Pizza

Tinkyáda® Brown Rice Pasta

Glutino® Pretzels and Crackers

Pocono® Cream of Buckwheat®
Hot Cereal

Barbara's® Cereals

Purely Elizabeth™ Granola

Horizon Cereals

Udi's™ Frozen Gluten-Free Bread

NadaMoo! Dairy-Free Ice Cream

Annie's® Gluten-Free Products

Now® Guar Gum

Lucy's® Cookies

Applegate® Corn Dogs
and Deli Meats

Menu Ideas

When I'm making up my menus for the week, I like to think about all the things I have going on and how many mouths I need to feed. Then I think about how much time I've got, and I make my list. Here are some of my more successful menus for entertaining and keeping the family fed.

Breakfast or Brunch

Repo Ron's Kuntry Omelet • 56
Baking Powder Biscuits (with salted butter) • 50
Frozen Fruit Salad • 116

Carolina Sausage Scramble • 43
Donna D's Honey'd Oat Bread • 58
Sun Tea Cake with preserves • 192

Apple Something Fritters • 47
Cheesy Bacon 'n' Corn Skillet Cakes • 57
My Morning Glory Muffins • 70

Countless Coconut Coffee Cake • 46
Lemon Poppy Seed Friendship Muffins • 44
Butter-Me-Up Deviled Eggs • 108
Fresh fruit and bacon

Lunch

Freestylin' Tacos • 81
Pepsi Peanut Pie • 190

Hush-up Spicy Hush Puppies • 92
Anytime Coleslaw • 85
Amy's Hot, I Mean Bra-Burning Hot, Wings • 82

Jessie-Mae's Meatball Po' Boys • 94
Root Beer Floats • 179

Tuna Melts • 128
Cold Macaroni Salad • 84
Honey Dew Cookies • 178

Carolina Pimiento Cheese Sandwiches • 74
Over-the-Sink BLT • 91
Orange Upside-Down Picnic Cake • 186

Suppertime

∽∾∼

Fancy Nancy's Crab Dip • 110
Jalapeño Shrimp and Cilantro Rice • 154
Lizard Limelight Atlantic Beach Pie • 180

Gluten-Free Hamburger Helper • 149
Three-Bean Salad • 161
Banana Puddin' • 172

Finger-Snappin' Split Pea Soup • 148
Alexa's Best Ever Meat Loaf • 140
Bourbon Sweet Potato Surprise • 153
Chess Pie • 171

Old-Timey Celery Soup • 139
Amy's Chex Crunchy Chicken Tenders • 151
Mashed Potatoes • 146
Late-Night Twinkies • 118

A Cheese Ball • 107
Tuna Tetrazzini Casserole • 144
Big green salad
1920 Miss American Pie • 168

Parties

String-Cheese Quesadillas • 127
Twice-Baked Spam-tatoes • 141
Corn Casserole • 78
Gluten-Free Butterscotch Crimpets • 177

Devils on Horseback • 115
Amy's Armadillo Eggs • 112
Crispy Corncob Cornbread • 156
Peachy Keen Slump • 188

Spinach Artichoke Dip Done Right • 114
Beef Tips with Rice • 142
Hominy Casserole • 138
Pecan-Crusted Pork Tenderloin • 158
Big green salad
Strawberry Cobbler • 166

Onion Dip • 121
DJ Silver's Spicy Fried Pickles • 106
Barbecue Shrimp • 76
Pepsi Peanut Pie • 190

Puredee Pretzel Bites • 120
Super Bowl Five-Layer Dip • 126
Quick Nachos • 122
Slice-and-Bake Chocolate Chip Cookies • 130
Mississippi Mud Bars • 184

Universal Conversion Chart

OVEN TEMPERATURE EQUIVALENTS

250°F = 120°C   400°F = 200°C

275°F = 135°C   425°F = 220°C

300°F = 150°C   450°F = 230°C

325°F = 160°C   475°F = 240°C

350°F = 180°C   500°F = 260°C

375°F = 190°C

MEASUREMENT EQUIVALENTS
Measurements should always be level unless directed otherwise.

⅛ teaspoon = 0.5 mL

¼ teaspoon = 1 mL

½ teaspoon = 2 mL

1 teaspoon = 5 mL

1 tablespoon = 3 teaspoons = ½ fluid ounce = 15 mL

2 tablespoons = ⅛ cup = 1 fluid ounce = 30 mL

4 tablespoons = ¼ cup = 2 fluid ounces = 60 mL

5⅓ tablespoons = ⅓ cup = 3 fluid ounces = 80 mL

8 tablespoons = ½ cup = 4 fluid ounces = 120 mL

10⅔ tablespoons = ⅔ cup = 5 fluid ounces = 160 mL

12 tablespoons = ¾ cup = 6 fluid ounces = 180 mL

16 tablespoons = 1 cup = 8 fluid ounces = 240 mL

About the Author

Amy Shirley is the costar of the number one truTV show *Lizard Lick Towing* and holds twenty-seven world, national, and state records in weightlifting. When she's not helping her husband, Ronnie, repossess a car, she's in the kitchen whipping up all kinds of gluten-free goodies. She lives in Lizard Lick, North Carolina, with Ronnie and their four children.